P9-CMW-600

1st ed.
20⁰⁰
Wis.

# THE
# SONGS
# MY
# PADDLE
# SINGS

# THE SONGS MY PADDLE SINGS

## NATIVE AMERICAN LEGENDS

COLLECTED BY
**JAMES RIORDAN**

ILLUSTRATED BY
**MICHAEL FOREMAN**

FOREWORD BY
**PRINCESS SHIRLEY LITTLE DOVE**

PAVILION

First published in Great Britain in 1996 by
**PAVILION BOOKS LIMITED**
26 Upper Ground, London SE1 9PD

Text copyright © James Riordan 1995
Illustrations copyright © Michael Foreman 1995

The moral right of the author and illustrator
has been asserted

Designed by Janet James

All rights reserved. No part of this publication
may be reproduced, stored in a retrieval system, or
transmitted, in any form or by any means, electronic,
mechanical, photocopying, recording or otherwise,
without the prior permission of the copyright holder.

A CIP catalogue record for this book is available
from the British Library.

ISBN 1 85793 244 7

Set in 11.5/17pt Dutch 823 by
Dorchester Typesetting Group Ltd
Printed in Italy by Graphicom

2 4 6 8 10 9 7 5 3 1

This book can be ordered direct from the publisher.
Please contact the Marketing Department. But try your
bookshop first.

# CONTENTS

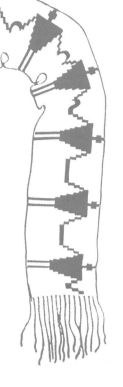

# FOREWORD

by

Shirley Little Dove Custalow McGowan

Stories in the Powhatan culture, as in all Native American cultures, were told to teach the new generation about our rich and honourable heritage, of our deep-rooted instincts and way of understanding and sharing the world and our place in it.

Stories taught respect and honour of people and everything Mother Earth had to offer. All living things were sacred to our people because the Great Spirit had created it so it was good and perfect. Our people knew the God of all creation and we knew our part in His creation.

Native American Indian children were taught respect and honour while still toddlers through the telling of stories. These stories provided unique and authentic sources of knowledge that children could relate to and from which they could learn important values about the world in which they lived.

This classic collection of Native American Indian stories has indeed expressed the heart of the Native American Indian people and demonstrates how knowledge, respect and honour was passed on through stories. I can only have deep respect for James Riordan, who spent so many years travelling in Canada and the United States, getting to know the native people from many different tribes as the four winds blow. This book does relate his deep care for such an ancient people.

NOTE:

Shirley 'Little Dove' Custalow McGowan is from the Mattaponi Reservation in the USA. The reservation, located near West Point, Virginia is home to the descendants of one of the original Powhatan tribes which greeted the English settlers who came to Jamestown with Captain John Smith in 1607.

Little Dove is the daughter of Chief Webster 'Little Eagle' Custalow, Chief of the Mattaponi Tribe. She was born and raised on the reservation, learning her ancestors' traditions and culture. She was given her mission as a child by her grandfather, a previous Chief of the Mattaponi Tribe, just before he passed on to the spirit world. That mission was to travel in all directions (as the four winds blow) with the history of her people. Also, that she must see non-Indian people through the Great Spirit's eyes and share her heritage with the Creator's love.

Shirley Little Dove asked the Great Spirit to open all doors she was ever to walk through and to give her wisdom, grace and knowledge that she would always represent her people with dignity, respect and honour. Little Dove travels sharing her rich heritage through Native American educational programmes in schools, museums and other organizations.

# INTRODUCTION

It was Christopher Columbus who gave the people of the New World the name *Indios*, and from this they were named by the English, 'Indians'. Later, the French added *peaux-rouges*, or 'redskins'. Columbus described these native people in a letter to the King and Queen of Spain:

> 'There is not a better nation in the world. They love their neighbours as themselves, they talk in sweet, gentle tones, and are ever smiling.'

Over the next four centuries, from 1492 to 1890, the Native American Indians found their lands invaded by several million Europeans. During that time, especially in the terrible thirty year span between 1860 and 1890, the culture and civilization of the Native American Indian were destroyed, and the victors sang their songs of white heroes, with the 'redskins' cast as villains.

Only rarely was the voice of the Native American Indian heard, and then almost always as recorded by the white man or woman. Yet the Native Indian voice is not lost; the original residents of America have found champions among some whites – such as Dee Brown in his history of the American West, *Bury my Heart at Wounded Knee*, or Kevin Costner in his beautiful film, *Dances with Wolves*, in addition to the many recorders of Native American legends.

My own interest in the American Indians began some twenty years ago when I began gathering tales from among the native peoples of North America, starting in Alaska and British Columbia. Then, over the next fifteen years, I journeyed eastward to Newfoundland, and southward through the US eastern seaboard, across Texas, New Mexico and Arizona to California and Nevada, dipping into Mexico. With the assistance of various American universities, I was able to make contact with members of nearby reservations and discover for myself the way of life and traditions, the customs and folklore of what were once called North America's Indian tribes. I learned to be patient, to observe propriety and, most importantly of all, to visit a reservation only after careful preparation through its members. Eventually, on occasion, I was fortunate enough not only to be an honoured guest at potlatches, but to record a large number of stories.

During my time in Ontario, I came across the folktale collection of an amazing woman, E. Pauline Johnson, or Tekahionwake, to give her the Mohawk name she preferred. She was the youngest child of an Englishwoman and a Mohawk chief, and she grew up to become a distinguished poet and collector of folktales. She was a tireless fighter for her people's cause, and in one of her most passionate poems, *A Cry from an Indian Wife*, she writes:

'Go forth, nor bend to greed of white man's hands,
By right, by birth, we Indians own these lands,

Though starved, crushed, plundered, lies our nation low;
Perhaps the white man's God has willed it so.'

We cannot undo the past. But we can recognize the truth of history and thus help to right a dreadful wrong. We can also contribute by returning to the native peoples their own culture. It was the very lack of a written language that helped to promote folktales, the sole means of expressing the ideas and aspirations of the tribes.

The Native Americans depended on imagery to express their thoughts, so that many translations of their stories fall flat on the printed page. Some of the best, however, provide a true understanding of their robust and poetic quality. For those brought up to think of Native Americans as savages it is a revelation to find words of beauty and reason and gentleness. More than that, we may learn something about our own relationship to the earth from a people who were true ecologists.

Writers and artists have been expressing the stories and legends of America's native peoples for centuries. Michael Foreman and I would not have attempted our task without first-hand acquaintance with our subject matter. You cannot depict a way of life and people without seeing, hearing, touching and feeling. This was our Golden Rule.

James Riordan

# THE MONTHS AND SEASONS

The tribes of North America had various ways of counting time. Some relied on changes in the season and growth of crops for guidance as to when their annual festivals and seasonal celebrations took place. Others fixed their festivals by phases of the moon and the habits of animals and birds. But most depended on the moon for marking the passage of time.

Many tribes measured their years by moons, giving them twelve lunar months, the year beginning at the first new moon after the spring equinox. To the Sioux, March was Worm Moon, April the Moon of Plants, May the Moon of Flowers, June the Hot Moon, July the Buck Moon, August the Sturgeon Moon, September the Corn Moon, October the Travelling Moon, November the Beaver Moon, December the Hunting Moon, January the Cold Moon, and February the Snow Moon. They had no division into weeks, but counted days by 'sleeps'.

A more exotic way of naming months was that used by tribes on the north-west coast of Canada and Alaska. Starting with January, there was the Moon of the Old Buck; Cold Udder Moon, Warm Udder Moon, Calving Moon, the Moon of Running Waters, Making Leaves Moon, the Moon of Warm Sunshine, Velvet Antlers Moon, the Moon of Love among the Reindeer, First Winter Moon, Muscles on Deer Back Moon, and Shrinking Days Moon.

Our stories feature the Ojibway/Chippewa 'Moon of Falling Leaves' (September), 'Moon when the Green Grass is High' (August), and 'Moon when Geese Shed Their Feathers' (May); the Seneca/Iroquois 'Moon when the Deer Paw the Ground' (April–May) and the Squamish 'Moon of the Greening Grass' (February–March).

*Call these fairy stories if you wish. They all have a reasonableness that must have originated in some mighty mind, and, better than that, they all tell of the Indian's faith in the survival of the best impulses of the human heart, and the ultimate extinction of the worst.*

E. PAULINE JOHNSON-TEKAHIONWAKE

# ONE

# CREATION OF THE WORLD

*This story of the world's creation is told by the Pueblo peoples,
so called because of their settled existence in villages, called
'pueblos' in Spanish. Their culture is found largely in the desert
areas of south-west America (Arizona and New Mexico).*

◆ In the beginning was Awonawilona – The-One-Who-Contains-All. Awonawilona was invisible, enshrouded in darkness and engulfed in emptiness.

Then, one time, out of Awonawilona rolled silvery mists and flowing streams. From the darkness Awonawilona now fashioned a fiery ball, the sun. And as the sun touched the billowing mists, they gathered together to form raindrops which became the ocean.

Next Awonawilona planted his seed upon the ocean's waters. Under the sun's warm caress the seed grew to form a green cover that spread across the waters until it hardened into a solid mass. This Awonawilona split into two: one half became Mother Earth, the other Father Sky.

Father Sky covered Mother Earth and life started to grow within her.

Mother Earth spat upon the sea and stirred it with her fingers until a foam arose. She breathed upon this foam and created black and white mists which floated as clouds above the ocean. Meanwhile, Father Sky breathed upon the clouds so that they dropped life-giving rain upon the earth.

Then, Father Sky held out his hand to reveal grains of shimmering corn – some silver, some gold – as numerous as the desert sands. With a flick of his wrist he flung the silver grains up into the heavens and they became the stars. The gold grains he gently placed upon the breasts of Mother Earth, saying, 'These golden grains shall be food for our children.' And when they had done these things, Father Sky and Mother Earth separated, and Father Sky rose into the heavens.

Life grew swiftly within Mother Earth and it was not long before she gave birth to the first living beings. But the creatures that emerged were ugly serpents, writhing from deep inside Mother Earth towards the light of day. Only one human being, Poshaiyangkyo – The-One-Alone – managed to escape from the earthly depths. As he emerged into the light he prayed for the release of his brothers and sisters still struggling inside the earth.

In response, Father Sky cast his seed once more upon the sea and out of the foam appeared giant twins who hurled thunderbolts that made deep holes in the earth. Binding trees, vines and grasses together, they then made a ladder so that the human prisoners could escape from the dark bowels of the earth.

Not all succeeded in climbing out. Some fell from the rope ladder and, with hideous screams, vanished into the dark abyss. They were later to be cast out by Mother Earth, some in the shape of fearful monsters that roamed the earth when it was young. The strongest and fittest of the humans, however, survived and came out into the upper world.

Once their eyes became accustomed to the light, these strong humans shrank back in terror, for all around them were scaly, slimy beasts that stalked across the barren, rocky surface, avoiding only the smoking volcanoes looming high into the sky. Surely the first humans could not survive in that inhospitable world? In despair, they sank to their knees and called upon Father Sky to save them.

Father Sky heard their pleas, and came to his children's aid. He made thunder roar and lightning flash, and sent down thunderbolts to destroy the terrible monsters. Meanwhile, his frightened children cowered

beneath whatever shelter they could find as the earth shook and trembled from the furious storm.

At last peace descended like a dove. The people cautiously emerged from their caves and looked about them: all around were the carcasses of dead beasts; the barren rocks were broken, the soil neatly furrowed and ready to receive the first corn seeds. The people began to till the earth and eat the harvest.

To this day the bones of those first monsters can sometimes be found; and, in the scorched, scarred rocks, they are a reminder of Father Sky's awesome power.

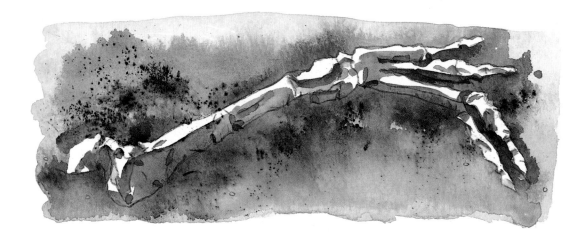

# TWO

# THE ORIGIN OF STORIES

*The people of the Seneca nation, from the lands around what is now Toronto, tell this legend of how the first stories came to be told.*

In a Seneca camp, close to Niagara Falls, there once lived a boy whose parents died when he was born. He was brought up by an aunt, who gave him the name Orphan Boy. And Orphan Boy grew up strong and wise. One day, in the Moon When the Deer Paw the Ground, Orphan Boy came of age, and his aunt gave him a bow and arrows, saying:

'It is time for you to learn to hunt. Go to the forest and bring back some meat.'

He set off early next morning, and very soon had good fortune: he shot three birds. At about midday, however, the sinew that held the feathers of his arrow together came loose, and Orphan Boy made for a clearing through the trees, where he sat down cross-legged upon a smooth, flat-topped stone to mend it.

All of a sudden he heard a deep voice:

'Shall I tell you a story?'

Orphan Boy glanced up, expecting to see a man standing there. Seeing no one, he looked all round the clearing before returning to his work.

'Shall I tell you a story?' came the voice again.

The boy was beginning to feel afraid. He peered in every direction, yet still could see nobody. Clearly, someone was playing tricks on him. He stopped his work to listen carefully, and when the voice called out again he found to his surprise that it was coming from the stone on which he sat.

'Shall I tell you a story?'

'What do you mean?' asked the boy. 'What are stories?'

'Stories are what happened in the long-ago time.'

'Then I would like to hear one,' said the boy.

'Only if you give me the three birds you have caught,' said the stone.

Orphan Boy gladly laid his birds upon the stone and sat back to listen in the quiet of the glade.

And the stone began.

'My stories are like the stars that never fade. There was a time when our people covered the entire land as the waves of a stormy sea cover the sandy seabed. But that time has long since gone, along with the greatness of our tribes.'

When the stone had finished one story, it began another. All the while the boy sat, head bowed, listening. Towards sundown, the stone suddenly said:

'We will rest now. Come again tomorrow and bring the people of your camp to listen to my stories. Tell each to bring a small gift.'

That evening the boy told the whole camp about the storytelling stone, and he gave them the stone's message. And so it was, early next morning, that the people followed him to the clearing. Each person put what he or she had brought – meat or bread or tobacco – upon the stone; and they all sat down.

When all was quiet the stone spoke:

'Now I shall tell you stories of what happened long ago. Some of you will remember every word I say, some only part, others will forget it all. Now listen closely.'

The people bent their heads and listened. Once in a while some said 'Uhn' and nodded. The stone told of how the moon got its shadow, how happiness came to the tribes, how sickness first arrived, why the grass whispers its secrets, how the first water lily appeared, and many other wonderful tales.

By the time it finished, the sun was almost down. The stone then said, 'My stories are all told. You must keep them as long as the world

has no end. Tell them to your children and your children's children, and so on, down the ages. And when you ask someone for a story, always give a gift, whatever you have. There, that is all, I have finished.'

And so it was. All the stories we know come from the stone, and from the stone came all the wisdom the people have.

# THREE

# THE DEEP WATERS

*People of the same nation would often exchange stories when
they visited friends and relations in other camps. This Creation story
was passed from one Squamish man to his 'tillicum' on
such a visit.*

◆ It was in the Moon of Greening Grass when I first heard this beautiful story of the Flood. My old tillicum had come from his camp to see me through the rains and mists of late winter days. The gateways of my wigwam always stood open for his feet to enter, and this special day he came with the worst downpour of the season, to where I was living, near Vancouver.

Helping him off with his greatcoat, I chatted to him about the deluge of rain, and he remarked it was not so very bad, as one could yet walk.

'Fortunately yes, for I cannot swim,' I told him.

He laughed, replying:

'Well, it is not so bad as when the Deep Waters covered the world.'

I saw a legend coming, so I crept into the shell of single sounds.

'No?' I said.

'No,' he replied. 'For one time there was no land at all. Everywhere there was just water.'

Then began the story.

It was after a long, long time of this rain. The mountain streams were swollen, the rivers choked, the sea began to rise. Yet still it rained, for weeks and weeks, while the mountain torrents thundered down, and the sea crept silently up. The level lands were first – they floated in sea water, then disappeared. The slopes were next to slip into the sea. The world was slowly being flooded. Hurriedly the Native tribes gathered together in a place of safety, far above the reach of the on-creeping sea. The spot was the circling shore of Lake Beautiful, up the North Arm. They held a Great Council and decided at once upon a plan of action. A giant canoe would be built, and it would be anchored in case the waters mounted to the heights. The men would work on the canoe, the women on the anchorage.

A giant tree was felled, and day and night the men toiled over its building into the biggest canoe the world had ever known. Not for an hour, not for a moment did the work stop; many worked while the weary ones slept, only to awake to renewed work.

Meanwhile, the women also worked at a rope – the longest, the strongest that Indian hands and teeth had ever made. Scores of them gathered and prepared the cedar fibre; scores of them plaited, rolled and seasoned it; scores of them chewed upon it inch by inch to make it soft; scores of them oiled and worked it to make it resist the sea.

And still the sea crept up and up and up.

It was the last day of the building; hope of life for the tribes, of land for the world, was ebbing fast. Strong hands fastened the rope the women had made – one end to the giant canoe, the other about an enormous boulder, a great immovable rock as firm as the foundations of the world – for might not the canoe, with its priceless cargo, drift far out to sea, and when the water subsided, might not this ship of safety be miles and miles beyond the sight of land on the storm-driven Pacific Ocean?

Then, with the bravest hearts that ever beat, willing hands lifted every child of the tribes into this vast canoe. Not one baby was overlooked. The canoe was stocked with food and fresh water. Lastly, the old men and women selected, as guardians to these children, the bravest, strongest and most handsome young man of the tribes, and the youngest and most beautiful mother in the camp – a girl of sixteen, with a baby of but two weeks

old – and placed them in the canoe, she at the bow to watch, he at the stern to guide, and all the little children in between.

And still the sea crept up and up and up.

At the crest of the bluffs about Lake Beautiful the doomed tribes crowded. Not a single person tried to enter the canoe. There was no wailing, no crying out for safety.

'Let the little children, the young mother and the bravest and best of our young men live,' was all the farewell those in the canoe heard as the waters engulfed the people, and the canoe floated. Last of all to be seen was the top of the tallest tree, then all was a world of water.

For days and days there was no land – just a rush of swirling, snarling sea. But the canoe rode safely at anchor, the rope which those scores of dead, faithful women had made, held as true as the hearts that beat behind the toil and labour of it all.

One morning at sunrise, far to the south, a speck floated on the breast of the waters. At midday it grew larger; at evening it was larger still. The moon rose, and in its magic light the man at the stern saw it was a patch of land. All night he watched it grow, and at daybreak he looked with happy eyes upon the summit of what is now called Mount Baker.

He cut the rope, grasped the paddle in his strong young hands, and steered towards it. When they landed, the waters had ebbed to half way down the mountainside. The children were lifted out, the beautiful young mother and the young brave turned to each other, clasped hands, looked into each other's eyes and smiled.

And down in the vast country that lies between Mount Baker and the Fraser River they made a new camp, built new lodges where the little children grew and thrived, and lived and loved, and the earth was renewed by them.

The Squamish say that in a big crevice half-way to the crest of Mount Baker may yet be seen the outline of a huge canoe.

The old tillicum ceased speaking, while the shadows of centuries gone crept into his eyes. Tales of the misty past always inspired him. And for a long time we both sat in silence, listening to the rains that were still beating against the window.

# FOUR

# GREAT SNOW IN THE NORTHLANDS

*The Slavey people from the shores of Great Slave Lake (in what is now Canada's North-West Territories) tell this story of the time when the animals, birds and fish lived in peace and friendship, before people appeared on earth.*

One night in this long-ago time, the darkness was very black and snow began to fall. It fell throughout the long, black night. The night seemed endless. The snow became deeper and deeper, covering plants and bushes; the animals had difficulty finding food, and many died.

At last their chief called a council.

'Let us send messengers to the Sky World,' the council decided. 'They will find out what is causing this long night and deep snow.'

So they sent as messengers one member of each family of animal, bird and fish that lived upon the shores of the Great Slave Lake. Those that could not fly were carried on the backs of those who could. So all entered through the trapdoor that led to the Sky World.

Beside the trapdoor stood a great lodge made of deer skins. And inside the lodge were three bear cubs. It was the home of Black Bear, an animal not known on earth at that time. Their mother, the cubs said, was in her canoe on the lake nearby, spearing Caribou.

The animals did not like the idea of Black Bear spearing Caribou, one of their own family. But they said nothing. Instead, they looked around the lodge. Hanging from the cross-bows overhead were some curious bags.

'What are in those bags?' they asked the cubs.

At first the cubs were silent. When asked again, they said reluctantly:

'We can't tell you. Wait until our mother comes back. She asked us to stay here and keep watch on them.'

'Perhaps those bags have something to do with us,' the earth animals wondered to themselves. So once again they asked the cubs about the bags.

Finally, the cubs confessed:

'This bag contains the winds. That one contains the rain. This one the cold. That one the fog. This one ...'

They would not say what was in the last bag.

The visitors felt sure that the last bag must contain the sunshine, and sunshine was what they wanted. So they left the lodge and held a council. They saw Black Bear landing her canoe on the far shore of the lake, and quickly they thought of a plan.

'Mouse, you go to Bear's canoe and gnaw a hole in her paddle close to the blade. When you have done this, signal to Caribou.

'Caribou, as soon as you get the signal, you jump into the lake and begin swimming. Before Black Bear comes close, swim ashore and run into the woods. The rest of us will hide until it is safe to take the bag of sunshine.'

Before the fox hid himself, he put his head inside the lodge, telling the the cubs:

'Keep a look out for Caribou. It may come near enough for you to call your mother.'

Meanwhile, Mouse ran to the far shore of the lake and gnawed a hole in the paddle. As soon as she signalled, Caribou jumped into the water.

At once the cubs saw him and yelled to their mother:

'Mother, Mother, look, Caribou!'

The earth animals, watching from their hiding places, saw Black Bear jump into her canoe, seize the paddle, and begin to row as hard as she could. Caribou also kept an eye on her as he swam. Soon, however, the paddle broke, the canoe turned over, and Black Bear vanished beneath the waters of the lake.

Caribou swam safely ashore, Mouse returned to her friends, and all the

earth animals ran into the lodge.
They pulled down the bag they wanted and inside
found the sun, moon and stars. These they
threw down through the trapdoor to the earth below.
When they looked down they could see the snow starting to
melt from the heat of the sun.
Thinking the earth world would soon be safe, the animals
began their flight down to earth. But some had
accidents on the way: Beaver split his tail, spilling spots of
blood over Lynx; Moose flattened his nose and
Buffalo bumped his back. Ever since that time, Beaver's
tail has been flat, Lynx has been spotted,
Moose has had a flat nose and Buffalo
has had a hump upon his back.

Also since that time there have been bears in the earth world, for the three cubs came down with the earth animals.

All the same, it was still hard to obtain food, because the snow melted so quickly it covered the earth with water. The fish who had been living on land found they could swim, and so they carried their friends upon their backs. Meanwhile, the ducks set to work to pull the land up from beneath the water.

At last the animals were so hungry that they sent Raven out to look for dry land. At that time Raven was the most beautiful of birds, but while looking for land he found the body of a dead animal. Although he had never before eaten anything except berries and willow leaves, he now began to eat the body of his animal brother. As punishment, he was changed into the ugly bird he is today. All the animals and birds hate him; and even man, who eats everything else, will not touch his flesh.

Then the people sent Ptarmigan out to look for dry land. When the bird came back he carried on his back a willow branch. It was a message of hope. As a reward, Ptarmigans turn white when the snow begins to fall in the Barren Land; thus they warn the animals and the people that winter is near.

But the peaceful and friendly life on the lake was no more. When the flood waters had gone, the fish found that they could no longer live on land; for if they did they would be eaten by the birds and the animals. The birds found that they were safer high in the trees and up in the mountains than anywhere else. Every animal chose the place that suited it best.

Soon the birds and fish and beasts could not even understand each other's language.

Not long afterwards the first human beings came to the lake.

Since then there has been no peace at all.

# FIVE

# LITTLE STAR

*The Blackfoot living on the plains of what is now Alberta and*
*British Columbia are also known as the Siksika nation;*
*they were called Blackfoot evidently because their moccasins were*
*blackened by the ashes of prairie fires.*

◆ Early one morning, as the Sun rose from his bed beyond the Rocky
Mountains, his handsome son, Morning Star, addressed him boldly:

'Father, I am tired of my lonely vigil in the sky. I wish to take a wife to
keep me company.'

'Is your mind made up, my son?' asked the Sun.

'I have looked down upon the tepees of the Blackfoot tribe and seen a
beautiful maid,' Morning Star replied. 'I love her dearly and wish her to
be my wife.'

His father shook his head.

'You cannot wed an earthly maid,' he said. 'She would bring unhappi-
ness on you and on herself. Her home is upon the earth. Should she dwell
in the skies she would sorely miss her people.'

Morning Star was very sad. He could not drive from his mind the
enchanting maid, Soatsaki. Each dawn he gazed down upon her from his
lofty home, as she slept within her father's tent. His longing grew, and

33

soon touched the tender heart of his mother, the silver Moon. She begged her husband to change his mind.

At last, reluctantly, the Sun gave in.

'But hear me well,' he said to Morning Star. 'Once she dwells within our realm she must never again look upon the Blackfoot lands, lest her heart be filled with longing to return.'

Morning Star was overjoyed. He painted his bronze body, stuck a red eagle's feather in his long black hair, and put on his scarlet cloak and shining black moccasins. Dressed and painted thus, he appeared before the maid he loved. Though she was startled to see the strange brave, she was quickly taken with his noble bearing. She fell in love herself, and gladly agreed to be his wife.

'Dear Soatsaki,' said the handsome brave, 'to marry me you must give up your earthly life. My tepee is in the skies. You must bid farewell to the people of your tribe forever.'

So in love was Soatsaki that she readily agreed to what he said. After parting with her family, she flew up to her new home with her husband, Morning Star.

The young brave and his wife were very happy and, in the space of several moons, a son was born. They called him Little Star.

One day, as Soatsaki sat in the Moon's tepee, nursing her infant son, she asked the Moon why it was that the big iron pot in the centre of their home always boiled without a fire.

'It has a source to fuel it,' said the Moon. 'But heed my words, daughter of the earth, you must never move that pot. If you do, great misfortune will befall you.'

Soatsaki thanked the Moon for her warning and gave her word she would not touch the pot.

Yet at midday, when the pale Moon was sleeping soundly, the lovely Indian maid could not restrain her curiosity. She approached the empty pot and tried to pull it to one side: she tugged and pushed until finally, with one great heave, she shifted it aside.

Well! Now she could see right through the hole beneath the pot. As she knelt down to take a better look, she saw her former home, the green border of the prairie with its shooting threads of gold, scarlet and blue, the blossoming wolf willow and dog rose. Her heart beat wildly as she recognised on the plain below the tepee clusters of her own Siksika tribe. And she was filled with an uncontrollable longing to see her kinsfolk once again.

When her husband came home, he noticed at once the downcast look upon his wife's lovely face and asked for the reason.

'If only I could see my people once again,' she sighed. 'I should be very happy. Though I am content here with you, my husband, and our infant son, I long to pay just one visit to my native land.'

Morning Star was hurt at these unexpected words, for he knew that his wife had broken her promise. When his father, the Sun, heard the news, he flew into a rage.

'You are unworthy of a place in our heavens,' he fumed at her. 'Go then back to earth from whence you come. And take your child with you. No more will you see your husband, Morning Star. That shall be your punishment for disobedience.'

Soatsaki and Little Star were wrapped up tightly in a caribou skin and lowered on a leather thong through the hole beneath the iron pot. But before they reached the earth, Little Star began to cry and forced his head out of the caribou skin. As he did so, the leather thong slid along his face leaving a deep cut, two fingers' length across.

In the course of time his face wound healed, though it left an ugly scar along one side. So disfigured was he that the other braves of the tribe gave him the name of Poia, Scarface. Even though he was daring and skilful in the hunt, bringing much glory to his tribe, the braves and maidens shunned him as if he was not of their breed. Even the little children taunted him as he passed by, calling:

'There goes Scarface, the ugly one!'

Meanwhile, his poor mother, Soatsaki, pined away for her lost husband and finally died of a broken heart, leaving her son all by himself. He grew up with no family or friends for company.

He walked alone.

The lonely years passed by and, when he came to manhood, Poia fell in love with the daughter of a neighbouring chief. She much admired his skill with bow and arrow and she deeply respected his strength in combat with the other braves, but she could not gaze upon his scarred, disfigured face without a shudder of disgust. So she refused him.

Now, it was rare indeed for a maid to refuse a brave's proposal. And Poia was wounded and ashamed. He could not show his face before the tribe without their scorn.

'I must find a way of reaching my grandfather, the Sun,' thought Scarface in his misery. 'Perhaps he will take pity on me and remove this blemish from my face.'

So he set out on a journey westwards towards the lofty snow-capped mountains. For many moons he walked, climbing the jagged peaks, crossing the swift rolling rivers, leaping over the moving ice floes, until finally he reached the end of the world, where the mighty waters meet the sky.

He sat down, exhausted, on the rocky shore and looked up at the Sun.

'O mighty Sun,' he cried, 'Father of my Father, Grandfather to Little Star. Hear me now, I pray thee. Show me a way up to the heavens, that I may come to seek your aid. My soul is troubled. I would rather go to the land of the spirits than to live on earth, bearing forever the name of Scarface.'

For three days and nights, Poia waited, never eating, never drinking. On the fourth day, just as dawn was breaking, he opened his eyes to see a path of light stretching before him: it led from where he sat right across the waters to the sky.

Great was his joy as he stepped upon the firm broad shaft of light and mounted it with fast-beating heart into the heavens.

But then, just as he reached the home where he was born, he saw some way off seven giant eagles attacking his dear father, Morning Star. In another moment they would surely have pecked out his eyes. Swiftly taking arrows from his quiver, Poia fitted them into his strong bow, one after the other, and shot all seven eagles. Morning Star was overjoyed to see his long-lost son and rushed to join him.

'You have passed the trial of courage, my bold son,' he said . 'Now I can take you to your grandfather the Sun.'

Mighty Sun did indeed take pity on his grandson and removed the ugly scar.

'From this time forth,' he pronounced, 'no one shall call you Poia, but Little Star, as you were first named. And since you have borne your ugliness so bravely, I shall reward you with this magic flute: it will charm the heart of all who hear its music. Return to earth, my grandson, and wed the maiden whom you love. Then, should you so desire, you may return with her to your birthplace in the skies.'

So Little Star went back to the plains and stood before the great tepee of the neighbouring chief. As soon as he played his magic flute, the chief's lovely daughter emerged enchanted, and fell deeply in love with the now handsome brave.

They were soon married and, after the wedding celebrations, went hand in hand to the sky abode of the Sun, the Moon and Morning Star. And there they remained to this very day.

If you look up at the evening sky, you can sometimes see the tepees of their many children in what some call the Milky Way.

# SIX

# THE FIRST WHITE WATER LILY

*The Chippewa nations, who tell this story, have their cultural roots in the central regions of Canada. Most made their homes near fresh-water lakes, so their stories often have a lakeside setting.*

◆ Long ago, in the dawning of the world, people and animals lived as friends. There was no winter, with its cold winds and snow. Flowers blossomed the whole year round, and the birds, whose plumage was brighter and more beautiful than today, filled the air with happy song. There was no war. There was no fear. For there was no cause for one to harm another.

Once in that peaceful time, there was a people that lived beside a lake (now called Lake Superior). The lake gave them fish to eat and water to drink and cook their food in.

By day the people worked, and played their games of hide-and-seek, catching balls and dancing. Of an evening they would gather at the lakeside to watch the stars. For stars, they thought, were the homes of all the people who had died. When it rained, they believed it was really tears falling from the tents up in the sky, for the Star People always cried when they were sad.

One night, as the people watched, a star brighter than all the others shone far away, at the edge of the dark night sky. Every night afterwards they watched, as it came closer, growing brighter all the time. Finally, unable to find a home, it hung above the people beside the lake, lighting

40

up the fading embers of their campfires as they prepared to sleep.

The people were afraid of the star. Sometimes at dusk it would hang above the heads of little children, as if wishing to play with them, but their frightened cries drove it away. It tried to join in the games of men, but they thought it was an evil spirit and fired their arrows at it. How it longed to join the dancing of the women, bobbing and gliding round and round; but their angry shouting kept it away.

The star was sad and lonely.

Among all the people, only one was unafraid of the shining star. That was Powomis, a little girl who lived in her parent's tent at one end of the lake. The star held no fear for her; she loved it with all her heart and never tired of playing in its bright rays.

The star seemed to love Powomis too, for whenever the girl went with her mother and father to the hills, or fishing in the lake, or picking berries in the woods, the star followed, lighting up the way. When she woke up at night, there was the star, just above her head. Many a time she wished to reach up and touch it, but it always kept out of reach.

All the other people wondered at the star's devotion. How surprised they were to see its twinkling light, guarding the little girl. And they noticed that since the star's appearance, her father would always return from fishing with a good catch; her mother never came home from the forest without a basketful of nuts or berries.

'The star must be a good spirit,' the people said.

After that they spoke of it with love; and no one feared it any more. All the same, it never left its first, faithful friend.

The Moon of the Falling Leaves came to the forest on the hill; and it was beautiful beyond compare. The maple tree was afire with colour, gleaming in the autumn sun, with every shade of gold, brown, red and yellow. The slender leaves of the sumac tree were like fiery scarlet tongues. And with the fall of leaves, the nuts and berries ripened.

It was then, one autumn morning, that Powomis took her little willow basket and went to the woods to gather fruit.

At the forest edges the berries had been mostly eaten by birds and deer. Powomis pressed on into the forest depths. But amid the tangled vines and creepers she lost her way, and soon found herself in the waters of a swamp. She was terribly afraid, and shouted loudly for her parents. But no one heard her cries, save the frogs and birds, who merely mocked her.

As darkness fell she realized that she was quite lost; she was walking deeper and deeper into the swamp. Now the water came up to her knees, and the mud tried to drag her down. Unable to find a way to safety she plunged on blindly through the swamp.

When it was completely dark she kept looking up, hoping to see the star she loved. But the sky was full of low black cloud; it would not let her shining star peep through. Soon drops of rain began to fall, and they grew and grew until, it seemed, all the spirits of the sky were crying.

The water in the swamp rose higher and higher, and soon swept poor Powomis off her feet. She bravely tried to keep her head above the swirling waters but they dragged her down and down and down.

Her body was carried to a river and, from there, down to the lake. She was never seen again. Only her little basket was washed up on the shore, by her parents' tent.

As the days went by, the loving star shone even more brightly above the campfires round the lake. It never stayed long in one place. It seemed so restless, as if searching for something it could not find. And then, one night, it disappeared.

It was not seen again for many moons. And then, one day in the Moon when the Green Grass is High, a young man was walking at dusk close by the swamp when, to his surprise, he saw a light flickering through the trees. It was so beautiful that he followed it on and on; but it led him so far into the swamp that he had to give up pursuit. He returned to the lake to tell the people of what he had seen.

Then an old wise woman explained the story.

'The light you saw,' she said, 'is a lonely star once driven from the sky. It now wanders the land looking for the little maid it loved.'

That night, as the young man slept, he had a dream. And in that dream he saw the star again, but this time it had a young man's face, with tears glistening on his cheeks. In a sad voice, the handsome star-man spoke these words:

'Do tell me where little Powomis is. If she still lives, I will come down to earth to marry her. If she is dead, I shall guard her spirit all my days. Give me a sign.'

When the young man woke up from his dream, he hurried from his tent and looked into the early morning sky. There was the star above him, blinking sadly as its silver light faded in the glowing pink of dawn. That day, the young man called a meeting of all the people beside the lake.

'The star asks for a sign to tell him if Powomis lives,' he said. And he told them of his dream.

The elders puffed upon their pipes and talked of what to do. At last it was decided: a crown of pink blossoms was to be thrown into the lake as a sign of the young girl's death. Thus the star would know.

And so it was done.

Poor star. When he gazed down that night he saw the ring of pink blossoms on the silver lake and he knew his love had drowned.

All night long he grieved and then, before the dawn, his mind was set.

'I shall be close to Powomis in the lake,' he sighed. 'I shall see the canoes of her people as they paddle by. The little children will be my companions as they swim past and play. I shall watch over the babies as they sleep in their cradles beside the lake.'

As he finished speaking, he floated gently down and spread himself upon the moonlit waters of the lake. He was happy to enter the home that bore the secret of his dead Powomis.

Next morning, as the people looked up at the sky, the star had gone. Yet when they looked into the lake, they saw a most beautiful white blossom cupped in dark green leaves.

It was the first white water lily.

# SEVEN

# WHY THE NORTH STAR STANDS STILL

*The Pahutes, an ancient people, once large and prosperous, lived
mostly in what is now the state of Utah. To the Pahutes, the
supreme gods are two brothers, Tobats and Shinoh.*

The sky is full of living things. The Pahute call them *poot-see* and others call them stars. They are as restless as the Pahutes themselves, travelling around the universe and leaving trails all over the sky. Some of the stars are birds who go away for a time to winter in warmer climes; some are animals hunting for better grass – Quan-ants the Eagle, Cooch the Buffalo, Tu-ee the Deer and Cab-i the Horse. The sky is their happy hunting ground; they travel in search of food and follow the good weather.

Yet there is one who does not travel. He is Qui-am-i Wintook, the North Star. He cannot travel, since there is no place he can go. Once he was Na-gah, the mountain sheep on earth. He was daring, brave and sure-footed. Shinob, the Great Spirit, was so proud of him that he hung great earrings on the sides of his head to make him look more grand.

Always Na-gah would be climbing, climbing, climbing. He hunted in the roughest, and highest mountains, and there he lived and was happy.

Once in the long-ago time, Na-gah found a high mountain with steep smooth sides, ending in a high sharp peak reaching up into the clouds. He looked up at that peak and said:

'I wonder what is up there? I will climb to the very top.'

He set out to find a way up. Around the mountain he walked, seeking a path; yet there was none – nothing but sheer cliffs all the way round. It was the very first mountain he could not climb.

He thought and thought; and the more he thought the more determined he was to find a way to the top. Shinob would surely be proud to see him standing on the very peak of such a mountain.

After searching for an age, he finally found a crack in the rock; but the crack went down into the earth, not up. So down he went; there was no other choice. He had not gone far when he came to a path that turned upwards, and he began to climb. Soon it grew so dark that he could not see: he stumbled into rocks which broke loose and rolled down beneath his feet. A terrible crashing rang through the mountain as the rolling rocks dashed themselves to pieces at the bottom. In the blackness he often slipped and cut his knees, and his courage began to waver. He had never experienced such blackness before.

Na-gah was soon very tired and decided to turn back.

'Upon the open cliffs I am not afraid,' he said to himself. 'But this dark hole fills me with fear. I must find a way out.'

But when he turned to go back down he found that loose rocks blocked his way; he could not return the way he had come. There was only one way to go – and that was up. He had to continue climbing until he emerged into the light.

After a long time he was able to make out a faint light above him; and he knew he was safe. When he finally emerged into the open, he found himself on the very top of the mountain. He could see great cliffs below him, all the way round. He had only a small platform to move around on, and to gaze down from this great height made him dizzy. Nowhere could he climb down on the outside; and the way back was blocked on the inside.

'Here I must die,' he sighed. 'But at least I have climbed the mountain.'

He found a little grass growing out of the crevices and some water in the rock holes. After he had eaten and drunk, he felt better.

About this time, Shinob was out walking across the sky and was surprised to see Na-gah stranded on the mountain peak.

'I will turn him into a *poot-see*,' said Shinob, 'and he can stand there

and shine for everyone to see. He will be a guide for all living things on earth and in the sky.'

And so it was. Na-gah became a star that every living thing can see and the only star that will always be found in the same place. Travellers can find their way by him, since unlike the other stars, he stands quite still. And because he is in the north sky, the people call him Qui-am-i Wintook Poot-see, the North Star.

There are other mountain sheep in the sky. They have seen Na-gah on top of the high mountain and try to join him; so they are always moving round and round the mountain, seeking the trail that leads to the top.

# EIGHT

# SPIRITS OF THE EVENING STAR

*This Blackfoot legend is set many decades in the past when
there was no winter with its cold blizzards, and when humans and
beasts lived together in peace and accord.*

One time in this long-ago world, there was a chief who had ten daughters, all as lovely as the moon. When they grew to women, nine daughters married young braves. But the youngest would not listen to the handsome braves who came to woo her; she would say:

'That one is too fat; he will never do.'

'Did you see how shabby his moccasins were?'

'I didn't like the way he spoke.'

One night, as the fire flickered low, a strange young warrior came to the door.

'Dah-joh,' said the mother, 'come inside.' But the visitor stood at the edge of the light and pointed his finger at the girl.

'I have come to take you for my wife,' he said.

Now this young man was very handsome. His face shone in the firelight. Above his waist was a fine wide belt of black and yellow wampum that glittered like sunlit water. On his head he wore two tall feathers and he moved with the grace of a willow tree bending with the wind.

How could the youngest daughter not fall in love with him? In no time at all they were married.

Now that all his daughters were wed, the old chief held a party for them and their husbands. And on the appointed day they all came to the father's lodge and sat down for the meal. During the feasting a voice, unheard by others, spoke to the handsome brave. It seemed to come down from the skies. Glancing up, he saw the Evening Star shining through the smoke hole of the lodge.

'My son,' the Star began, 'you may come to live with me and bring all your relatives as well; you shall have all that you desire.'

All at once the lodge rose into the air. As it floated upwards the wooden bark changed to the gossamer wings of a million tiny creatures. And as the young chief gazed upon his wife he saw that her buckskin dress was now of shining satin, and the string band tying her hair became a silver feather. The father, mother, sisters and their menfolk had turned into brightly-coloured birds; some were jays and some were parrots, some were orioles and parakeets. And all sang most wonderfully.

Up, up sailed the lodge until it reached the Evening Star where all was silvery white and tranquil. How happy the Star was to see his son.

As the birds flew joyfully about the Star, the son sat down at his father's feet with his young wife at his side. The father welcomed them into his home and they lived happily together until eventually a son was born.

As the boy grew up he yearned to hunt and shoot with bows and arrows, and since the Evening Star loved his little grandson he taught him all the skills of hunting; but he gave a solemn warning:

'On no account must you shoot a bird; woe betide you if you do.'

For many days the little brave shot his arrows into the air, at trees and shrubs and blades of silver grass. But he soon tired of this sport and longed to fire at a moving bird. So, when no one was looking, he aimed his arrows at the birds; they were much harder to hit than a standing tree. One day, however, he crept up behind an oriole and caught it unawares. He let loose an arrow that flew straight and true, and it sank deep into the oriole's breast.

How proud he was of his success!

Imagine his surprise when the bird turned into a young girl with an arrow sticking from her breast. It was one of his mother's sisters who now took her earthly form. No sooner had her red blood touched the ground than the spell was broken.

The young brave felt himself slowly falling though the sky until at last his feet touched earth and he found himself on a mountain top, high above the plains. As he looked up he saw his aunts and uncles floating down towards him; soon they, too, were standing safe and sound upon the rocky mountain. Then came the silvery lodge, its walls shimmering with the gossamer wings of tiny creatures; it landed gently on the rock, and out stepped his parents.

All had now regained their earthly form, but not entirely as before: for they were all no bigger than butterflies. They had become mountain spirits.

The mountain top which had been bare before now grew a carpet of feather grass sprinkled with brightly-coloured blooms, with blue pools of water here and there.

The spirits were happy to have their earthly home and thanked the Evening Star. His kind gaze bathed them all in starlight and they heard him softly say:

'Be happy, little children, I shall watch over you from the sky.'

From that time on they lived together in happiness. Of a warm summer evening they would gather by the lodge to dance and sing and gaze up at the stars.

And when the moon is shining brightly you too may see the silvery lodge upon the mountain top. And you may also, if you listen closely, hear the singing of the Spirits of the Evening Star.

# NINE

# LONE BIRD

*Before the white man came, the Chippewa were one of the*
*greatest of the Native Indian nations. Their tales, such as this one, describe*
*the lands where they prospered: the forests around the Great Lakes*
*where they hunted deer and the rivers and streams where they caught fish.*

Many snows in the past, when the Chippewa were as numerous as leaves upon the maple tree, there lived on the shores of the big water, now called Lake Superior, a young girl whose name was Lone Bird. She was the only child of She Eagle and Dawn of Day. No daughter of the tribe was as proud and strong as she: she was as graceful as the silver birch tree, tall and slender, her voice was like the river's song. From all the camps of the Chippewa nation young braves would come to seek her hand and ask to take her from her parents' lodge. But she looked coldly on them all. In vain they sang to her of their skill as hunters, of their daring in battle. In vain they brought gifts to the lodge of She Eagle and Dawn of Day.

The girl's heart, they said, was like the winter's ice.

Her father tried to breathe warmth into his daughter's heart. He praised the skill and courage of the young braves he knew and trusted; no maid of the tribe had so noble a band of suitors from which to choose.

But Lone Bird took his hand in hers. She smiled as she said:

'Do I not have my parents' love? Do I not have you to protect me? What need have I to wed?'

Dawn of Day made no reply. The next day he went from his lodge, summoned young braves of the camp, and told them of his plan.

'All you who wish to marry my daughter should gather at the lakeside. There you will run a race. He who is fleetest of foot shall win my daughter and take her to his lodge.'

At the father's words, the young men's hearts were filled with joy. Eagerly, each brave prepared for the coming race; and each hoped for the deer's nimbleness of foot.

News of the contest spread through all the camps, and braves came from far and near. On the morning of the race, a great throng gathered upon the shore. All had come to see who would win the beautiful Lone Bird. The young braves were there, painted in finest colours and plumed with feathers of the eagle and the turkey cock.

Only one member of the tribe was missing – Lone Bird. She sat in her parents' lodge, weeping.

When all was ready for the race, the braves lined up, bronze muscles rippling in the sun and hearts pounding like war drums. At the signal, they all rushed forward in a jostling throng.

Soon two runners had broken free of the racing pack. They were Bending Bow and Hunter of Deer. Both had loved Lone Bird for many moons. Each was as fleet-footed as a deer, as swift as the rushing wind. Neither could outstrip the other, and when they reached the finishing line, the judges could not tell which brave had won.

So Bending Bow and Hunter of Deer raced again. And once more they came in, side by side. A third time they ran, and no victor was declared.

'Let them jump against each other,' someone said.

Yet when they jumped, neither could beat the other by a hairsbreadth.

'Let them display their hunting skill,' the elders said.

So the next day at dawn, Bending Bow and Hunter of Deer set off across the plain. On their return, each threw down the skins of ten bears and twenty wolves.

The elders muttered amongst themselves, and an anxious buzz went round the tribe: it was clear that the spirits had been at work. Lone Bird's father, Dawn of Day, returned to his lodge with troubled mind. There sat his daughter, with head bowed, eyes red with weeping, knuckles white on trembling hands. His heart bled, for he dearly loved his only child.

Lifting her head, he gently said to her, 'Do not weep, daughter. Every man must have a wife, every wife a man.'

'Dear father,' she replied, 'but what if I do not wish it so?'

Sadly, he returned to the elders gathered beside the lake.

'The race is at an end,' he said. 'Bending Bow and Hunter of Deer have done well; but it seems the spirits are against our plan. My daughter shall remain unwed.'

And so, dismayed, the braves returned to their camps.

Summer and autumn passed, and the cold winds of winter blew across the lake. Then, one spring, when the chokeberries were ripe, when the days were warm enough for boys to swim in the melted snow water, Dawn of Day went to Maple-Syrup Hill to make sugar from the sap of maple trees. As always, Lone Bird went along to gather the sweet liquid in birch-bark bowls. By and by, as smoke was curling from her father's fire, she sat upon a rock and glanced around. The sun was warm and bright, the air was filled with the scent of fir and pine; yet somehow Lone Bird felt sad. Her thoughts were of her parents, of their silver hair and stumbling steps; their journey to the Happy Hunting Grounds was not far off.

'What will become of me when they are gone?' she thought. 'I have no brother or sister, no children of my own, no one to share my tent.'

And for the first time she felt the chill hand of loneliness grip her heart. As she gazed down the slope at the early snowdrops pushing their frail heads through the margin of the snow, she saw that they grew in clusters, like small families. As she watched the birds busily building nests, she saw that they too did not live alone. Just then she heard the whirring of a flock of wild geese swooping across the lake. They landed in a furrow upon the water and glided away in pairs.

'No flowers, no birds, not even wild geese live alone,' she murmured to herself.

Her lonely thoughts made her sadder still. She recalled her coldness to the braves who used to court her; none came any more. She recalled her father's efforts to find her a husband; he had long since let her be.

'Yet still I am glad I did not wed,' she sighed.

For a long time she sat upon the rock above the lake, wrapped in her

gloomy thoughts. When she rose to go, it was already dusk and the full round moon made a silvery path across the lake. Lone Bird gazed up longingly at the bright moon in the sky and, stretching forth her arms, she cried:

'Oh, how beautiful you are. If only I had you to love I would not be lonely.'

The spirits heard the cry of the lonely maid and carried her up to the moon.

Meanwhile, her father finished his work upon the slopes and went back home without his daughter, who was nowhere to be seen. When he did not find her in the lodge he returned to Maple Syrup Hill, and from there he called her name:

'Lone Bird! Lone Bird!'

Time and again he called, but no answer came.

His anxious eyes searched the trees, the slopes, the waters of the lake. Then, in despair, he glanced up to the sky, towards the brightly shining moon. Could it be? Yes, there was no doubt. He could clearly see his daughter smiling down, held in the moon's pale arms.

She seemed to say she was content.

No longer did he grieve. No longer did She Eagle or Dawn of Day worry about their daughter's fate. They knew she would be cared for by the loving moon.

Many, many moons have passed since the days of Lone Bird and her Chippewa tribe. Their people have become weak and few; their tents are scattered to the winds. White strangers occupy their hunting grounds and the graves of their dead go untended.

Yet the flowers still bloom in springtime; birds still build their nests; wild geese fly and the stars still shine. And if you look up at the moon, you can still see the face of Lone Bird smiling down. She gives hope to her people as they tell her story by their fading fires.

# TEN

# WHISPERING GRASS

*According to Ojibway legend, there is an area of land around
what is now Lake Superior where all animals can find shelter from the
hunter's arrow. This is the story of the animals' friend.*

◆ Once, many long years ago, there was a green hill covered in long grass which whispered and sang as the wind blew through it. The grass was a friend to all animals, especially the wild deer, the grey wolf and the white fox.

One summer's day Whispering Grass grew very excited. The south wind had brought it strange news, which meant great danger to the animals, and the Grass wished to send a message of warning to them.

So she called to the butterflies and told them to go at once to the deer, the wolf and the fox, summoning them to the green hill. Away flew the butterflies, and it was not long before all the animals were gathering to hear what this message might be.

'Listen, my brothers,' murmured Whispering Grass. 'There is great danger for you this day, for across the prairie comes a band of hunters to kill you.'

'Hunters? What are hunters?' asked the animals.

'They are people with bows and arrows,' replied the Grass, '– deadly arrows that will pierce your hearts. The hunters are quite close and once they see you they will kill you.

'What can we do?' asked the animals, alarmed. 'You are wise, Whispering Grass; tell us what we may do to save ourselves.'

'Go to your homes,' answered the Grass, 'and remain there until sundown tomorrow. If all is safe, I shall send my messengers, the butterflies, to summon you here.'

The animals did as they were commanded, and by the time the hunters reached the foot of the green hill, there was nothing to be seen but dainty butterflies hovering above the Grass. For the rest of the day the hunters searched for game in the hills, yet not a single deer could they see, not a wolf, nor a fox. Late afternoon, they returned, empty-handed, to their camp at the foot of the hill. They were tired and hungry, for they had brought no food with them: they had expected to find plenty of game.

'Let us go home,' said one hunter. 'There is no game in this land and I am hungry.'

'No,' said the second hunter. 'Let us wait until tomorrow. Perhaps we'll see game then.'

'Yes, let us wait,' said a third hunter. 'Tonight we shall eat grass. See, the hill is well covered with grass. If the animals eat it, why cannot we?'

'But it is Whispering Grass,' said the first hunter in a low voice. 'He who eats Whispering Grass can no longer kill anything with his arrows.'

'No, brother,' said the second hunter. 'It is not Whispering Grass. Listen, there is a west wind blowing through it, and yet we can hear no sound of whispering.'

They all listened keenly. And as the second hunter had said, there was no sound of whispering. The wind was waving the Grass and bending its blades low. Not a sound came from them.

'You are right, it is not Whispering Grass after all,' said the first hunter. 'I am starving. Let us eat.'

So they all gathered many handfuls of the Grass and put it into a pot. They boiled it until it was soft, then, gathering about the pot, they ate the Grass with much relish. After that, they rolled themselves in their deerskins and soon fell asleep.

It was now the sunset hour. So, calling the butterflies to her, Whispering Grass gave them a message for the animals.

'Go to your brothers,' she said, 'and tell them all is safe now. At sunrise tomorrow morning they may leave their homes and wander among the

hills. Their enemies, the hunters, will try to shoot them with their arrows, but they need have no fear, for now those arrows will not touch them.'

The butterflies flew away quickly and passed on the message to the deer, the wolf and the fox.

At sunrise next morning the animals left their hiding places. They had not gone far when they saw the hunters coming towards them. Remembering the message of their friend, Whispering Grass, they had no fear at all, and soon saw that the Grass was right. The hunters fired their arrows, yet each one flew through the air and fell harmlessly at their feet.

All day long the hunters stalked their prey and loosed their arrows and each time the arrows failed to hit their targets. At last, tired and dispirited, the men went back to their camp at the foot of the green hill.

'My brothers,' said the first hunter, 'that was indeed Whispering Grass which we ate last night. See, all day our arrows have failed to find their mark, though the game is plentiful.'

'Why did the Grass not whisper then?' asked the second hunter. 'It deceived us.'

'Yes, it deceived us,' said the third hunter. 'It held its peace while we listened, so that we might be tempted to eat it. Now we have lost our power of hunting and will be mocked by other hunters.'

'We must destroy Whispering Grass,' said the first hunter. 'Let us go and pull it up by the roots so that never again will it be able to cheat men.'

'Let us wait until the moon is high in the sky,' said the second hunter. 'then we can uproot all the Grass and leave the green hill bare and brown.'

The butterflies, who had been hovering nearby, heard what the men were saying and now flew to the animals to tell them the news.

'Oh, my brothers,' said the butterflies, 'your enemies, the hunters, have planned to kill Whispering Grass tonight. You must save her.'

'We will save her,' said the deer. 'Whispering Grass is our friend; she saved our lives.'

Turning to the fox, the deer said:

'Oh, brother, you are wise. Can you not think of a plan to save the Grass?'

'I am not wise enough for that,' said the fox. 'But I know of someone who is very wise. You, my brothers, stay here while I run with all speed to the Dark Hills where the Manitou of Bright Fire lives. He is wise and great and will help us.'

So saying, the fox ran towards a long range of hills, and it was not long before he reached a small opening in a hill which led underground. On entering, he found himself in a long tunnel at the end of which he could see a red light. He went on until he found himself in a large, low cavern in the centre of which a bright red fire glowed. He could see, in its light, a dark figure seated on the floor. The figure turned towards him, and the fox saw the kind features of the Manitou of Bright Fire.

'You have come to me for help,' said the Manitou in a deep, soft voice. 'What is wrong, brother?'

'Our friend, Whispering Grass, is going to be torn up by the roots tonight,' said the fox. 'Can you tell us how to save her, for she has been kind, and saved us from the hunters?'

'My brother,' said the Manitou, 'do you see these things that resemble dark stones?'

He pointed to where a heap of black pebbles was lying on the cavern floor.

'I have gathered these from the bowels of the earth. Many years ago Gitche Manitou, the Mighty Spirit, took pieces of the midnight sky and mixed a million sunbeams with each one. Then he hid them deep in the earth where people would find them when they needed heat and light. I shall place some of these black stones in my fire, while you return to your brothers, wolf and deer. Bid them return with you, and when you again reach my cave the stones will be ready for you. Now go, and waste no time, for you must have everything done before the hunters awake.'

The fox needed no second bidding. Away he went like the wind. The deer and the wolf were anxiously waiting for him. Quickly giving them the Manitou's message, he ran back with them to the cavern where they found the Manitou had placed a number of the black stones in his fire; they were soon bright red and glowing.

'My children,' said the Manitou, 'take these burning coals and put them in a circle on the hillside among the Whispering Grass. They will not harm the Grass and their heat will not burn you as you journey back. But henceforth, mark my words: always beware of a glowing fire, for I can give you my protection this once only.'

The animals seized as many of the burning coals as they could carry and raced back towards the hill. The night was dark, as the moon had not yet risen, and when at length they reached the green hill, they saw that the hunters were still sleeping. As the Manitou had instructed, they put the coals in a circle on the hillside, and then they hid behind some trees.

Scarcely had they done so when the hunters awoke. At once they noticed the strange, glowing circle on the side of the hill. They rubbed their eyes and stared again: it was still there, burning and yet with no flame. They trembled and shook, not daring to go near it. At last one hunter said;

'My brothers, let us return to our village. This Whispering Grass must be a friend of Gitche Manitou and we have done wrong to eat it.'

'You are right, my brother,' said the other hunter. 'We will return and tell our brothers of this terrible warning that Gitche Manitou has sent us.'

So saying, they turned and disappeared swiftly into the darkness, while the circle on the hillside glowed brightly until the sun rose. When daylight came there was nothing to be seen of the black stones, yet where they had been there was a wide brown circle which could be seen quite plainly from the valley.

The circle is there to this day. Yet as you climb the hill the circle vanishes, and not a patch of burnt grass can be seen. There is another thing; from that night onwards the animals have been afraid of glowing fire, for

they know the Manitou cannot give them his protection.

All the same, he has been their greatest friend ever since. When they are in trouble they go to the Dark Hills and, creeping through the long tunnel, they reach the cavern where the bright fire glows. There they tell the kind Manitou all their troubles, and he does his best to comfort them.

In the autumn he tells the deer where to hide in the hills, so that the hunters cannot reach him. In the long, cold winter he tells the hungry wolf where to find food, and in the summer he shows the white fox how to double back on his trail so that none may catch him.

And to all of them he has taught the secret of the glowing fire, that its brightness spells danger, save when they rest beside it in his cavern underneath the Dark Hills.

# ELEVEN

# HIAWATHA, UNITER OF THE IROQUOIS

*For most of us, the name Hiawatha is associated with the hero of
Longfellow's poem: the legendary figure, based largely on Ojibway
stories. The real Hiawatha was of the Mohawk nation; he was
the one who founded the Five Nations of the Iroquois, uniting the
Mohawk, Seneca, Onondaga, Oneida and Cayuga.*

◆ The Great Spirit of Life, weary of the wars and bloodshed that were
slowly destroying his earthly children, called a council to which he invited braves from all the tribes: from the Blackfoot in the west to the
Mohawk in the east.

In a voice like thunder he scolded them for their constant strife. He
ranted and raged until, finally, his tone changed.

'My children,' he said, 'I tell you this: henceforth you must agree to a
truce. You must share peacefully the lands I have given you to hunt, the
streams I have granted you to fish, the marshes that are yours to catch
duck and goose. One day soon I shall send you a wise medicine man who
will live among you and show you the ways of peace. Heed his words and
you will grow and prosper; ignore him and you will all melt away as the
snows in spring. There, I have spoken.'

Years passed and the wise medicine man did not come. The truce
agreed by the tribes following the great council expired and they forgot the
Spirit's warning: once again they began to kill each other.

But the medicine man did appear. His name was Hy-ent-wat-ha, the
Comber-Out-Of-Snakes, whom we know as Hiawatha. We shall learn later
how he came to get his strange name.

No earthquake, no trailing comet marked his birth. He grew up like all young braves of his Mohawk tribe: he knew nothing of the lands beyond the world of what is now called New York State. One day in early manhood, however, he had a dream of the future given to him by the Great Spirit. This vision was of a world without war, where tribe was at peace with tribe, where each person was strong in *orenda* or spirit, where life was governed by justice and mercy.

Like all good men, Hiawatha tried to plant the seed of his vision in others by his own example; and his reputation spread through the tribes as someone who could move people by his words, his enthusiasm, his ability to speak with the spirits.

But the Great Spirit did not hold full sway over the lives of his children. He always had to contend with the ruler of the Underworld, an evil Spirit who took the shape of an ugly, twisted creature with claws for hands and feet, and writhing snakes for hair. His name was Atotarho and he was the much-feared medicine man of the Onondaga tribe.

The contest between Hiawatha and Atotarho, between good and evil, now began. At first Atotarho's medicine was stronger and Hiawatha was hard-pressed. First he lost his dear wife Wanutha, struck down by an arrow sent by Atotarho; then, one by one, his daughters died from some mysterious disease. Finally, his own people, seeing how helpless he was, rejected him and drove him out. So Hiawatha wandered from tribe to tribe, still vainly preaching his ideas of love and peace.

Although evil had by now spread like thistles through an untended cornfield, Hiawatha soon possessed a strong weapon with which to combat it. For one night he had another vision, this time of a giant spruce tree whose summit pierced the sky and reached into the land of the Great Spirit. It became known as the Tree-That-Lights-Up-The-World, for its branches came to represent the unity of all the tribes, firmly rooted in the great strong trunk. Right at the top perched a giant eagle, keeping watch against enemies who might break the peace.

Just as fire sweeps through grasses parched by the sun's fierce heat, Hiawatha's energy, fanned by his vision of the giant spruce tree, now spread quickly through the tribes. One by one, the tribes of the Iroquois –

first the Mohawk, then the Oneida, the Cayuga and the Seneca – were converted to the idea of a league of the Iroquois tribes, to be called Ho-de-no-sau-nee. All that remained outside the League was the Onondaga under their evil medicine man, Atotarho.

Once more, Hiawatha journeyed into Onondaga territory. After three suns had crossed the sky, he found himself seated around a council fire in the Onondaga camp. The firelight lit up hostile faces, and eyes that gleamed like those of hungry wolves through the flickering shadows of the night. Most sinister and hateful of all was Atotarho, who seemed to be transformed into a hundred different shapes by the firelight shadows; upon his head the snakes writhed and wrapped their slimy coils in a seething mass, hissing and flicking their tongues at Hiawatha.

Yet Hiawatha, undaunted, rose to address the assembly. The pictures in words he painted were as colourful as the scarlets and golds and russets of the autumn maple leaves. His firm voice shattered the silence of the night. He depicted scenes of wanton destruction, of brother slaying brother, of Iroquois lifeblood draining away into the blood-soaked soil. So enfeebled would the Iroquois soon become that their common foe would break them as easily as snapping dry twigs for fire.

Finally, inspired by his noble vision, his voice rising to a roar, he told them of the Tree-That-Lights-Up-The-World, symbol of the League of the Five Nations of Iroquois tribes. The League would end all wars among the brother nations and form the rock on which they could build a great union of all the tribes, from the eastern sea to the mountains of the sunset.

'Our League shall have a council of fifty sachems or elders from the five tribes,' he said. 'And since women are the source of life and are therefore most interested in preserving peace, they shall choose those sachems.'

To the men and women of the Onondaga tribe, Hiawatha had a special message:

'The council's meeting place shall be here, for you form the centre of Iroquois land: the Onondaga shall be the keeper of the sacred fire, a fire that shall burn forever as a symbol of the light of peace.'

His audience muttered among themselves, yet still was unconvinced.

Then came his final words which were to stun them all.

'And we shall accept Atotarho as our Sachem Chief.'

At that a great murmur went up. Like aspen leaves which rustle and wave before the breeze, so the heads of the Onondaga leaders now rose and fell in excited consultation. At last Atotarho spoke:

'We accept the terms. We join our brothers in the great Ho-de-no-sau-nee. We shall be keepers of the sacred fire.'

At once, runners were sent to the other tribes, summoning their sachems to the founding ceremony of the new union of tribes. And when everyone had gathered and the fifty sachems had been solemnly installed, there remained only the crowning of Atotarho as Sachem Chief.

Holding the sacred deer antlers, Hiawatha slowly advanced towards Atotarho standing before the great assembly. And Hiawatha spoke these words, the oath of office of the Iroquois Constitution:

'We now crown you with the sacred emblem of the antlers, the sign of your office. You shall become the teacher of our people in the Five Nations. The thickness of your skin shall be seven spans, for you shall be unyielding to anger, rude offence or unfair criticism. You shall do your duty with infinite patience, and your firmness shall be tempered with tenderness for your people. Neither anger, nor fear shall find a place in your heart, and all your words and actions shall be marked by calm deliberation. In all your official actions, self-interest shall always be cast aside; you shall look and listen for the welfare of all your people and always bear in mind the interests of the future generation, the unborn of the Nation.'

As the antlers were placed upon Atotarho's head, a gasp of astonishment went up. For the snakes fell to the ground, writhing in agony; then they shrivelled and died. Atotarho's twisted body turned into a handsome, upright figure, the claws changed to human hands and feet.

Good had conquered evil. And from that day on, Atotarho, the Sachem Chief, devoted himself to the cause of peace and friendship among the five nations.

As for Hiawatha, The-Comber-Out-Of-Snakes, as he was now known, he spent the rest of his days carrying the message of peace and brotherhood to all the tribes throughout the continent. Tirelessly he paddled his sacred white canoe up and down the streams and seas until one day he set out on a voyage from which he never returned.

As he was journeying towards the setting sun, Gadowaas, the Guardian of Souls, took from his wampum belt the most brilliant star of all – the constellation we call the Milky Way – and tied it to Hiawatha's belt to light his way. It guided him to the land beyond the sunset where peace always reigns, and the children of the Great Spirit live in harmony amid deep meadows and shady forest glades surrounded by the summer sea.

To this day an empty seat is left at Iroquois councils: it is kept for Hiawatha whose spirit still guides the braves, ever counselling them on the ways of peace and brotherhood.

# TWELVE

# THE APACHE CINDERELLA

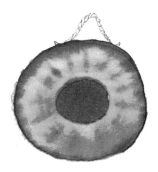

*Many years ago, the Apaches lived in a land of high red*
*mountains – the land which is now the Grand Canyon in Arizona.*
*The Apaches believed that they were protected by the Yei gods*
*who dwelt among them in mountain caves that were warm in*
*winter, cool in summer and dry when everywhere else was wet in*
*the rainy season.*

◆ In a cave high above the great canyon, the Chief Yei, Talking God, lived with his sister. Now, Talking God was invisible to all but his sister, and since he could mingle unseen and listen to people talking, he knew all human affairs, and was also a great hunter.

Many girls wished to become the wife of such a mighty god, and they would constantly crowd about the entrance to his cave. Talking God soon grew weary of this attention, so he let it be known that he would only marry the girl who saw him as he returned home at dusk. He knew that only the pure of heart and spirit would pass the test.

Many tried, but none succeeded. Each evening, as the sun went down, his sister would invite a girl to the cave and together they would look out for her brother as he climbed the mountain. When Talking God entered the cave he would take off his cloak and moccasins, handing them to his sister; at once they became visible. And as he sat down to eat, the waiting maiden would see food taken from the bowl and disappear into thin air. But she never saw Talking God.

Then the sister would ask:

'Can you see Talking God?'

'Oh yes,' the girl would lie.

And the sister would ask:

'With what was he pulling his sledge as he came up the mountainside?'

Each girl would guess as best she could.

'With an antelope hide.'

'With a coyote's tail.'

'With a long pole.'

The sister would put another question:

'Of what are his bowstring and arrows made?'

'Of the gut of rabbit, chipmunk, prairie dog …

With turkey, quail, sage hen feathers …'

Many tried, many lied. All failed the test. In turn, each maiden hoping to marry Talking God was sent away, disappointed.

Now there lived in the cave village a widower with his three daughters. The youngest girl was small and frail and gentle, well loved by all for her hard work and kindness to others. This made her two older sisters jealous, and they were unkind and cruel towards her. One day, when their father was away hunting, they tore the young girl's clothes so that she was dressed only in rags, cut off her long black plaits, and burned her face and arms with hot cinders from the fire, so that she was badly scarred. Thereafter the people called her Scarface.

When her father asked who had treated her so cruelly, the girl kept silent; but her sisters told him she had fallen asleep by the fire and fallen into the cinders.

Like other girls in the village, the two eldest sisters decided to try their luck with Talking God. So they put on their finest clothes, brushed their hair until it shone and went to Talking God's hogan. As he came up the mountainside, his sister asked, as usual:

'Do you see him?'

'Oh yes, yes, of course,' each replied.

Then Talking God's sister asked, 'With what is he pulling his sledge?' and each, guessing, answered separately,

'With rawhide.'

'With a wooden shaft.'

At that the sister sent them packing.

Soon after, little Scarface decided to try her luck; she was the only young maid who had not presented herself to Talking God. She patched up her tattered rags as best she could with bark from trees, decorated them with mud-paint, in the style of long ago, stuck a turkey feather in her hair and tied a squirrel tail about her head. Then, putting on her father's old moccasins, which were far too big for her, she left for Talking God's hogan.

As she climbed the hill, her sisters called after her,

'Why should he marry an urchin like you?'

And as she passed by other caves, children called her names: 'Scarface!' 'Tatters!'

She truly was a pitiful sight, with her strange clothes, short hair and disfigured face.

All the same, she was received kindly by Talking God's sister, for the woman understood far more than ordinary beings and could see the goodness of her heart. The two women stood waiting beside the cave entrance as the dove-grey evening sky turned to purple and the invisible hunter made his way home, up the mountainside, drawing the sledge behind him and holding his bow in one hand.

'Do you see him?' asked the sister, as he drew near.

'Yes, I do,' answered the girl truthfully.

'How strong and handsome he is.'

The sister was not surprised, for many girls had answered thus.

'With what is he pulling his sledge?' she asked.

The girl was silent for a moment, then answered boldly,

'With the Rainbow.'

The sister smiled.

Then she asked the second question:

'Of what is his bowstring made?'

Straightaway the girl replied, 'His bowstring is Kachinas, the path of the spirits, which others call the Milky Way.'

'So you *do* see him,' the sister said. 'You must truly be pure of heart and spirit.'

And she took the young girl into the cave and bathed her in a tub of warm water until all the scars disappeared from her face and arms; her hair grew long and black like the raven's wing; and she was given fine clothes and rich jewelry to wear. Then she was told:

'Take the place of honour, right next to the master's seat at the entrance to our home. For only you are fit to be his wife.'

Soon Talking God entered the cave and sat down beside her, proud to have such a beautiful young bride.

As for the girl's two sisters, they were punished for their cruelty. Talking God turned them into aspen trees. Ever since that day the aspen's leaves tremble in envy of their sister and in fear of the fury of the gods.

# THIRTEEN

# KINAK THE GIANT

*High above the Horton River in Canada's North-West Territories*
*tower icy mountains where, according to Inuit legend, a*
*race of giants lives. These giants are so tall their heads are hidden in the*
*clouds; they cross rivers and hills in a single stride and their cold*
*breath whistles through the drifting snow in wintertime. Yet, despite their size,*
*the giants are gentle creatures and often kind to those in need.*

One time, the woman Tayune was walking alone across the tundra when she chanced to meet a giant. It happened in mid-winter; she was fleeing from her husband whose cruel blows often left her black and blue. Finally, she made up her mind to leave him and, one night, while her husband slept, she crept quietly out into the snow. Better to die in the snow's cold embrace than from her husband's blows.

All that night and following day she stumbled through the snow, her face set against the driving wind. Her little stock of food was soon gone and hunger drove her to swallow handfuls of snow.

Just when she could bear her hunger no more, she came upon a cache of caribou meat, half-hidden in the snow. She could hardly believe her luck! Clearly, the meat had been left by hunters who planned to return later to claim their spoils. She looked all about, but could not see a soul.

'I am sure no one would mind me taking a little food,' she thought.

Gathering a few sticks, she made a fire in the shelter of a nearby hill and roasted some meat. When she had eaten her fill, she felt strong enough to move on; she stuffed a pouch with the remaining food and set off up the hill.

As she glanced about her she wondered at the hill's strange shape: it was just like a human foot, with five big mounds upon its crest – like a giant's toes. By the time she reached the top it was growing dark and she stopped to rest for the night.

She made a bed for herself between two mounds of snow and settled down to sleep. It was surprisingly warm and cosy, and she slept soundly till dawn.

For the next three days she journeyed down a gentle slope that led towards the north. Each night she found a warm place to rest. The first night she sheltered beneath an overhanging rock; on the second she sank into a deep hollow in the ground; and on the third, she found a dense, dark forest that provided protection from the wind.

Next morning, however, just as she was about to leave, a great booming voice came from somewhere overhead,

'Who are you? What brings you here?'

In terror, the woman stared about; then she understood! For the past
few days she had been walking along a giant's sleeping body. First she had
slept between his toes; then beneath his knee and in his navel, and now in
his thick beard!

Almost fainting with fright, she stammered out,

'My name is Tayune; I left home to escape my husband who beats me
all the time.'

The deep voice spoke again,

'You are welcome to stay here for as long as you wish. But I must warn
you of one thing: do not come close to my mouth, for if I cough or sneeze
you would be blown away.'

When she saw that the giant meant her no harm, her fears died away.

'You must be hungry after your long journey,' the giant said. 'I'll bring
you something to eat.'

Suddenly the sky grew dark and the woman saw a big dark cloud coming down. She drew back in alarm – but it was only the giant's hand, bearing meat which he put at her feet.

'You may build a fire from my beard,' he said in a kindly voice. 'I shall
not miss a few grey hairs.'

When she had finished her meal, the giant spoke again. 'Some frost has
got into my lungs in the night; I'll have to cough to clear it out. Hide inside
my bushy beard and hang on tight.'

Tayune clung firmly to the giant's beard as she heard a rumbling roar
and a fierce rushing overhead; a snowstorm raged beyond the beard.

'Pardon me,' the giant said.

And the sky grew clear once more.

As the days went by, Tayune and the giant became good friends. He
explained that his name was Kinak, and she should live beside his nose,
well away from his mouth; she could build herself a hut from hairs taken
from his beard.

She never lacked for food, since the giant only had to stretch out his

hand to catch a caribou or seal, whatever took his fancy. He also caught fox and wolf and bear so that she could make warm clothes, and line her home.

Thus they lived happily for some time. Now and then the woman's thoughts turned to home. Did her husband miss her? Was he sorry for driving her away? Kinak noticed her troubled frown and one day asked if she would like to return home.

'I do miss my home,' she said. 'But I'm afraid of my husband beating me again.'

'Have no fear,' the giant said. 'I will protect you: if ever you are in danger, just call my name.'

Kinak told her to cut off the ear tips of all the furs and put them in her pouch. That done, she stood before his lips as he instructed. All at once, there came a great blast of wind and she felt herself flying through the air; only when her feet touched the ground in her own camp did the wind drop and disappear.

Tayune's husband was sitting by the fire as she entered the hut. At first he thought she was a ghost, for he had long given her up for dead. But when he heard her story he welcomed her back and vowed never to beat her again.

Next morning, when he looked inside his store, he was amazed to find it full to bursting with rich furs. Each ear tip she had brought had turned overnight into a complete animal fur. In no time at all her husband sold the furs and became a wealthy man. For several years he kept the vow to his wife, mindful of her gift. But his wealth finally brought him to drink and his evil ways returned.

One day, he flew into a rage and went to beat her with a club; she fled from the hut, but he caught her in the snow and knocked her to the ground. As he raised his arm to strike again, she cried out in despair,

'Kinak, help me!'

At once the skies grew dark and a blinding blizzard blew up. The man was lifted up in a whirlwind and driven through the air until he was out of sight. Gradually, the storm died down and all was still once more. She never saw her cruel husband again.

Yet he did not die in the storm. The giant Kinak saw to that. He let the husband live in his beard, just as his wife had done. He repeated the warning not to approach his mouth.

But the man did not obey. He made up his mind to explore the place – perhaps he could find some wealth inside. Pushing his way through the dense forest of the giant's beard he suddenly came into the light. He was right by Kinak's mouth.

Just at that moment, the giant's lips opened wide and a fierce gust of wind burst out. Although the man tried to cling to the tangled hair, the gale was too strong; he was hurled far across the sky and vanished beyond the clouds forever.

Since that day Kinak has not been seen; nor has anyone dared seek him out. The Inuit know, however, that he still lives in the north, for on winter nights they can feel his icy breath and hear him whistling in the wind.

# FOURTEEN

# THE BEAR MAN

*There was once a boy of the Pawnee nation, settled in what is now
called Oklahoma, who would imitate the ways of the bear.
When he played with the other boys of his village he pretended to
be a bear; he even told them he could turn himself into a bear
whenever he liked. He came to act this way because of his father;
and this is his story.*

Before the boy was born, his father had gone hunting not far from the
camp, and had come upon a wounded bear cub. The tiny furry creature
was so helpless that the man could not pass by and let it die. So he stooped
down and tied some Indian tobacco round its neck, saying:

'The Great Spirit, Tirawa, will take care of you. This tobacco charm
will help you. I hope, in turn, that your fellow bears will one day take care
of my son when he is born, and help him grow into a great and wise man.'

With that he left the bear cub and returned to the camp.

He told his wife of the encounter with the bear cub: how he had looked
into its eyes and talked to it. Now, there is a Pawnee superstition that,
before a child is born, the child's parents must not look at an animal or
think too much about it, or else the child will inherit its ways. And when
the boy was born his habits resembled those of a bear; he became more
and more like a bear as he grew older.

He would frequently wander into the forest by himself and pray to the
Great Bear Spirit.

When he had grown to manhood, he led a Pawnee war party against
their enemies the Sioux. Unsuspecting, however, they walked straight into
an ambush and were killed, every last man of them.

Now, that part of the country was rocky and full of cedar trees, with many bear dens round about. It was not long before some bears came upon the dead bodies, and discovered that of the Bear Man. A she-bear recognized it at once as that of the man who had prayed to the Bear Spirit, sacrificed tobacco to them, made up songs about them, and had done them many a good turn.

She collected the remains of the Bear Man, whose body had been strewn across the plain; placing all the parts together, she lay down upon his body and worked her medicine on him until he showed signs of life. At length he recovered enough to be led, still very weak, to the she-bear's den.

During his time with the bears he was taught all the things they knew – which was a great deal, for the people know that the bear is the wisest of animals. The bears told him that all he had learned was the gift of Tirawa, who had made the bears and given them their strength and wisdom. He was instructed never to forget the bears, nor cease to imitate them, for that would determine his success as a wise and powerful leader.

Finally, the she-bear told him this:

'The cedar tree shall be your protector. It never grows old, is ever fresh and green, it is Tirawa's gift. If a thunderstorm comes while you are at home with your family, throw some cedar wood upon the fire and you will all be safe.'

When he arrived home, the young man was greeted with joy and astonishment, for everyone thought he had died with the rest of the war party. He at once told the tribe of how the bears had saved him and next day he took gifts of tobacco, beads, buffalo meat and sweet-smelling clay, to present to them. The she-bear hugged him and spoke these words:

'As my fur has touched you, you will be great. As my hands have touched you, you will be fearless. As my mouth touches your mouth, you will be wise.'

With that they parted for the last time.

In the passing of time, the Bear Man did indeed become the greatest warrior of his tribe. He was the originator of the Bear Dance which the Pawnees still practice to this day.

# FIFTEEN

# THE TULAMEEN TRAIL

*The people of the Nicola country tell this sad story about
a young girl's spirit, held forever in the Tulameen River which winds
through their land.*

Have you ever been through the valley lands of the Okanagan, the Nicola and the Similkameen countries? Have you ever listened to the call of the Skiikum Chuck, as the Chinooks call the tumbling streams that sing their way through the canyons with a music so sweet, so insistent that for many moons the echo of it lingers in your ears, and you will in all the years to come hear the voices of those mountain rivers calling you to return?

But the most haunting of all the melodies is the warbling laughter of the Tulameen River. Its delicate note is far more powerful, more far-reaching than the throaty thunders of Niagara Falls. That is because the Tulameen carries the spirit of a young girl held in its winding course, a spirit that can never free itself from the canyons to rise above the heights and follow its fellows to the Happy Hunting Grounds, but entwines its laughter, its sobbing, its lonely whispers, its even lonelier call for companionship, with the wild music of the waters that sing forever beneath the western stars.

Above all the sounds is the voice of the restless Tulameen as it dances and laughs through the rocky throat of the canyon, three hundred feet below. The Tulameen is as beautiful to look at as to listen to, with its rapids and showers of waterfalls, and it is here, where the trail winds about and above it for miles, that the Indians say it caught the spirit of the maiden.

It happened in one of the terrible battles that raged between the valley tribes before the white man's footprints were seen along these trails. None can now tell the cause of this warfare, but it was probably for tribal supremacy – that primeval instinct which assails the savage in both man and beast, that drives the hill-men to bloodshed and the leaders of buffalo herds to conflict.

This war of the valley tribes lasted many years: men fought, and women mourned, and children wept as all have done since time began. At last, each tribe nominated its leaders to decide the outcome. It seemed an unequal battle, for the old, war-tried Squamish chief and his two strong sons were pitted against a single Tulameen brave. Both sides had their loyal followers, both were strong in courage and wisdom, both were determined, and both were skilled fighters. But on the older man's side were experience and two other wary brains to help him, while on the younger's side was but the advantage of splendid youth and unconquerable persistence.

At every battle, at every skirmish, at every single-handed conflict the younger man gained little by little, the older man lost step by step. The experience of age was gradually giving way to the strength and enthusiasm of youth. Then, one day, they met face to face and alone – the old, war-scarred chief, the young battle-inspired brave. It was an unequal combat. And at the close of a brief but violent struggle the younger had brought the older to his knees. Standing over him with upheld knife, the Tulameen brave cried:

'Would you, my enemy, have this victory as your own? If so, I give it to you. But in return for my surrender I demand your daughter.'

For an instant the old chief looked in wonderment at his conqueror. He thought of his daughter only as a child who played about the forest trails or sat obediently beside her mother in the lodge, stitching her moccasins or weaving little baskets.

'My daughter!' he cried. 'My daughter, who is barely out of her own cradle basket! Should I give her to you, you whose hands are stained with blood, with the killing of a score of my tribe? You ask for this?'

'I do not ask it,' replied the young brave. 'I demand it. I have seen the girl and I shall have her.'

The old chief sprang to his feet and spat out his refusal.

'Keep your victory,' he said, 'and I shall keep my daughter.'

He knew he was not only defying his enemy, but defying death as well. The Tulameen laughed lightly.

'I shall not kill the father of my future wife,' he taunted. 'We must have one more battle, then your girl child will come to me.'

The brave made his proud way up the trail, while the old chief walked with slow and springless steps down into the canyon.

Next morning, the chief's daughter was walking along the heights, listening to the singing river, and sometimes leaning over the precipices to watch its curling eddies and dancing waterfalls. All of a sudden, she heard a slight rustle, as though some passing bird's wing had cleft the air. Then at her feet there fell a slender arrow. It fell with spent force, and her knowledge of the hunter's skill told her it had been shot to her, not at her.

She started like a wild animal. Then her quick eye caught the outline of

a handsome, erect figure standing on the heights across the river. She did not know him as her father's enemy. She only saw him to be young, strong and very handsome. The spirit of love awoke in her. Quickly she fitted one of her own dainty arrows to the bow string and sent it winging across the narrow canyon; it fell at his feet, and he, too, knew she had shot it to him, not at him.

Next morning, she crept noiselessly to the brink of the heights. Would she see him again, that handsome brave? Would he send another arrow to her?

She had not yet emerged from the table of forest before the arrow fell, its faint-winged flight heralding its coming. Near the feathered end was tied a tassel of ermine tails. She took from her wrist a string of shell beads, fastened it to one of her little arrows, and winged it across the canyon, as she had done the day before.

Next morning, before leaving the lodge, she fastened the tassel of ermine tails in her straight black hair. Would he see them? Yet something more precious than an arrow awaited her at the precipice. He himself was there, he who had never left her thoughts since that first arrow came to her from his bow string. His eyes burned with warm fires, but his lips said simply:

'I have crossed the Tulameen River.'

Together they stood, side by side, and looked down at the depths before them, watching in silence the little torrent playing over its boulders and crags.

'That is my country,' he said, looking across the river. 'This is the country of your father and your brothers; they are my enemies. I return to my own shore tonight. Will you come with me?'

She looked up into his handsome face. So this was her father's foe – the dreaded Tulameen!

'Will you come?' he repeated.

'I will,' she whispered.

It was in the light of the moon and through the kindly night that he led her down the steep precipice to the river's edge, and far up the rocky shores to the narrow belt of quiet waters, where they crossed in silence into his own land.

A week, a month, a long golden summer slipped by, but the old chief and his angry sons failed to find her. Then, one morning, as the lovers were walking together on the heights above the upper reaches of the river, even Tulameen's ever-watchful eyes failed to notice the lurking enemy. Across the narrow canyon crouched the two brothers of the girl wife. Their arrows were on their bow strings, their hearts on fire with hatred and vengeance. Like two evil-winged birds of prey those arrows sped across the laughing river.

Yet before they could pierce the breast of her Tulameen lover the girl moved in front of him, unsuspecting. With a little sigh, she slipped into his arms, her brothers' arrows buried in her soft, brown flesh.

It was many a moon before the Tulameen's avenging hand succeeded in slaying the old chief and his two sons. But when this deed was finally done, the handsome young Tulameen left his tribe and his country, heading into the far north.

'For,' he said, as he sang his farewell song, 'my heart lies dead in the Tulameen River.'

But the spirit of his girl wife still sings through the canyon, its song blending with the music of that sweetest-voiced river in all the valleys of the Dry Belt. That is why this laughter, the sobbing murmur of the beautiful Tulameen, will haunt for evermore the ear that has once listened to its song.

# SIXTEEN

# TWINS

*The Squamish used to believe that the birth of twins brought
disaster to the entire nation. This story tells how the ancient
Native lore was changed.*

◆ It was a grey morning when they told him of the disaster that had
befallen him. He was a great chief and he ruled many tribes on the North
Pacific Coast. But what was his greatness now? His young wife had borne
him twins, and she was sobbing out her anguish in the little fir-bark lodge
near the tidewater.

Beyond the doorway gathered many old Squamish men and women –
old in years, old in wisdom, old in the lore and learning of their nation.
Some wept, some chanted solemnly the song of their lost hopes and happiness, which would never return because of this tragedy. Others dis-
cussed the event in hushed voices, and for hours their grave council was
broken only by the infant cries of the two boy babies in the bark lodge, the
hopeless sobs of the young mother, the agonized moans of the grief-strick-
en chief, their father.

'Something terrible will happen to the tribe,' said the old men in
council.

'Something terrible will happen to my husband,' wept the young mother.

'Something terrible will happen to us all,' echoed the unhappy father.

Then an old medicine man arose, lifting his arms, with outstretched
palms to hush the lamenting throng. His voice shook with the weight of

many winters, yet his eyes were still keen, mirroring his thoughts, just as the still trout-pools in the Capilano Hills mirror the mountain tops. His words were firm, his shoulders straight and broad. His was an authority that no one dared dispute and his judgement was accepted as the words fell slowly, like rain upon the earth.

'It is the ancient law of the Squamish tribe that, should this evil befall them, the father of the twin children must go far away, into the mountains; there by his loneliness he must prove himself stronger than the evil, he must destroy the invisible foe that would otherwise follow him and all his people. In the course of time he will know by some sign in nature that his tribe is saved. He must depart before this sun sets, taking with him only his strongest bow, his fleetest arrows; and he must remain ten days alone up in the mountains.'

The firm voice ceased, the tribe wailed their assent, the father arose without a word, his drawn face revealing his agony over this seemingly brief banishment. He took leave of his sobbing wife, of the two tiny souls that were his sons, he grasped his favourite bow and arrows, and faced the forest like a warrior.

At the end of ten days he did not return, nor even after ten weeks or ten months.

'He is dead,' wept the mother into the ears of her two boys. 'He could not battle against the evil that threatens us. It was stronger than he – he who was so strong, so proud, so brave.'

'He is dead,' echoed the people. Our strong, brave chief is dead.'

So they mourned the long year through. But their chants and their tears only renewed their grief. He did not return.

Meanwhile, far up the Capilano, the banished chief had built his solitary home. Who can tell what trick of sound, what current of air, what faltering note in the medicine man's voice had deceived his alert ears? Yet some unhappy fate had led him to understand that his solitude must be for ten years, not ten full days, and he had accepted the word as binding. Had he refused, then evil would fall upon his tribe.

'It is fitting that I should suffer for my people,' he believed, as all his brothers and sisters of the tribe would agree.

With his hunting knife he stripped bark from firs and cedars, building for himself a lodge beside the Capilano River, where leaping trout and salmon could be speared by arrow heads fastened to long poles. All through the salmon run he smoked and dried the fish with great care. The mountain sheep and goats, and even the huge black and cinnamon bears, fell before his unerring arrows. The fleet-footed deer never returned from their evening drinking at the waterside, for their agile bodies were stilled when he took aim. Smoked hams and saddles hung in rows from the cross poles of his bark lodge, and the pelts of animals carpeted his floors, padded his couch and clothed his body. He tanned the soft doe-hides, making leggings, moccasins and shirts, stitching them together with deer sinew as he had seen his mother do long ago. He gathered the pale pink salmon berries, their juice a healthy change from meat and fish.

Month by month, year by year he sat beside his lonely camp fire, waiting for his long term of loneliness to end. One comfort alone was his – he was enduring the disaster, fighting the evil, so that his tribe might go unharmed, so that his people would be saved.

Slowly the tenth year dawned, and day by day it dragged its long weeks across his aching heart, for nature had not yet given the sign that he could return.

Then, one hot summer day, the Thunder Bird came crashing through the mountains about him. Up from the arms of the Pacific rolled the storm cloud, and the Thunder Bird, with eyes of flashing light, beat its huge wings on crag and canyon.

Upstream, a tall shaft of granite reared up, and there the Squamish chief crouched when the storm cloud broke and bellowed through the ranges, and on its summit the Thunder Bird perched, its great wings threshing the air into booming sounds.

But when the beating of those black wings ceased and the echo of their thunder waves died down into the depths of the canyon, the Squamish chief arose as a new man. The shadow on his soul had lifted, the fears of evil were beaten back and conquered. In his brain, his blood, his veins, his sinews, he felt that the poison of his grief dwelt no more. He had purged his guilt of fathering twin children; he had obeyed the law of his tribe.

He knew that the Thunder Bird, too, was dead, for its soul had left its body, and had appeared in the sky. It was a radiant semi-circle of glorious colour spanning from peak to peak and he could see it arching overhead, before it took its long journey to the Happy Hunting Grounds. He lifted his head then, for he knew it was the sign the old medicine man had foretold – the sign that his long banishment was over.

Through all those years, down in the tidewater country, the young twins were asking 'Where is our father? Why have we no father like the other boys?' They were met by the oft-repeated reply:

'Your father is no more. Your father, the great chief, is dead.'

But some strange intuition told the boys that their father would return some day. Often they voiced this feeling to their mother, but she would only weep and say that not even the great medicine man could bring him back.

When they were ten years old the two children came to their mother, hand in hand. They were armed with their little hunting knives, their salmon spears, their tiny bows and arrows.

'We go to find our father,' they said.

'You go in vain,' wailed the mother.

'You go in vain,' echoed the tribespeople.

But the great medicine man said:

'The heart of a child has invisible eyes; perhaps the child eyes see him. The heart of a child has invisible ears; perhaps those ears hear him call. Let them go.'

So the children went into the forest. Their little feet flew as though on

wings, their young hearts pointed to the north as does the white man's compass. Day after day they journeyed upstream; rounding a sudden bend, they saw a bark lodge with a thin blue curl of smoke drifting from its roof.

'It is our father's lodge,' they said, for their hearts were unerring in response to the call of their blood. Hand in hand they approached and, entering the lodge, they said one word:

'Come.'

The great Squamish chief stretched out his arms towards them, then towards the laughing river, then towards the mountains.

'Welcome, my sons,' he said. 'And farewell, my mountains, my brothers, my crags and my canyons.'

And with a child clinging to each hand he faced once more the country of the tidewater.

# SEVENTEEN

# THE TWO SISTERS

*There are two mountains close to the north-west coast of British
Columbia known by the Coast Salish as the Two Sisters.
The Salish believe it is to them we owe the Great Peace in which
we live, and this is their story.*

You may see them as you look towards the north and the west, where
the dream hills swim into the sky amid their ever-drifting clouds of pearl
and grey. They catch the earliest hint of sunrise, they hold the last colour
of sunset. They are twin mountains lifting their peaks above the fairest valley in all the land.

Sometimes the smoke of forest fires blurs them until they gleam like
opals in the purple air. Sometimes the slanting rains festoon scarves of
mist about their crests and the peaks fade into shadowy outlines, forever
melting into the distance. But for most days in the year the sun circles the
twin glories with a sweep of gold and the moon washes them with a torrent of silver. Often, when the valley is shrouded in rain, the sun turns
their snows to a deep orange. Through sun and shadow they stand immovable, smiling westward above the waters of the restless Pacific, eastward
above the beauty of Capilano Canyon.

Many thousands of years ago, there were no sentinels guarding the
outposts of this sunset coast. They were placed there long after the first
creation, when the Sagalie Tyee moulded the mountains and patterned the
mighty rivers where the salmon run, because of his love for his children
and his wisdom for their needs.

And in that long ago time a great Tyee had two daughters who grew to womanhood at the same springtime, when the first great run of salmon thronged the rivers and the ollallie bushes were heavy with blossoms. These two daughters were young and very beautiful. Their father, the great Tyee, prepared a feast such as the Coast Indians had never seen. There were to be days and days of rejoicing, the people were to come from afar, bringing gifts for the chief's daughters.

The only shadow on the joy of it all was that the tribe of the great Tyee was at war with the Upper Coast tribes in the north. Giant war-canoes slipped along the entire coast, war-parties paddled up and down, war-songs broke the silences of the nights, hatred, vengeance, strife festered everywhere, like sores on the body of the earth.

But the great Tyee, after warring for many weeks, turned and laughed at the battle and the bloodshed, for he had been victor in every battle, and he could well afford to leave the strife for a week and feast in his daughters' honour; he would not permit mere enemies to come between him and the traditions of his race. So he turned deaf ears to the war-cries; he ignored the paddle-dips that encroached upon his own coast waters, and he prepared, as a great Tyee should, to entertain his tribe in honour of his daughters.

Yet seven suns before the great feast, the chief's two daughters came before him, hand clasped in hand.

'O, our Father,' they said, 'may we speak?'

'Speak, my daughters, my girls with the eyes of early spring, the hearts of early summer.'

'Some day we will mother a man child who may grow to be just as powerful a Tyee as you. And for this honour that will some day be ours we have come to ask a favour.'

'It is your privilege at this celebration to receive any favour your hearts may wish,' he replied, placing his hand upon his heart.

'Then we wish you to invite the great northern tribe, the tribe you make war upon, to our feast,' they said fearlessly.

The chief was taken aback.

'To a peaceful feast, a feast to honour women?' he exclaimed.

'So we would desire,' they answered.

The chief was silent for a time. Then he looked upon his twin daughters and smiled.

'So then shall it be,' he declared. 'I can deny you nothing on this day. And in time you may bear sons to bless this peace you seek.'

Then he turned to the young men of the tribe and commanded:

'Build fires at sunset on all the coast headlands – fires of welcome. Man your canoes and face the north, greet the foe, and tell them that I, the Tyee of the Capilanos, ask that they join me for a great feast to honour my two daughters.'

When the northern tribe received this invitation they flocked down the coast to the feast of Great Peace. They brought their women and children;

they brought game and fish, gold and white stone beads, baskets and carved ladles, and wonderful woven blankets to lay at the feet of the great Tyee.

And he, in turn, gave such a potlatch that nothing in our history can compare with it. There were long happy days of merrymaking, long happy nights of dancing and camp-fires, and great quantities of food. The war canoes were emptied of their deadly weapons and filled with the daily salmon catch. The hostile war songs ceased and in their place were heard the soft shuffle of dancing feet, the lilting voices of the women, the games of the children of the two great nations which had been ancient enemies until now. For a lasting brotherhood was sealed between them.

Then the Sagalie Tyee smiled on his children.

'I will make these young-eyed maidens immortal,' he said.

In the cup of his hands he lifted the chief's two daughters and set them down in a high place, for they had borne two offspring – Peace and Brotherhood – each of which is now a great Tyee ruling this land.

And on the mountain crest above the place the palefaces call Vancouver can still be seen the chief's daughters wrapped in the suns, the snows, the stars of all seasons. They have stood in this high place for thousands of years and will stand for thousands more to come, guarding the peace of the Pacific Coast and the quiet of Capilano Canyon.

# EIGHTEEN

# SIWASH ROCK

*The Squamish tell this legend about the landmark, Siwash Rock,
which can be seen to this day in Stanley Park, Vancouver.*

It was thousands of years ago, before the white man came, that a handsome boy chief journeyed in his canoe to the upper coast for the shy little northern girl whom he then brought home as his wife. Boy though he was, the young chief had proved himself to be an excellent fighter, a fearless hunter, and a courageous man amongst the men. His tribe loved him, his enemies respected him, and the mean and cowardly feared him.

The customs of his ancestors were dear to him, the sayings and advice of the old people were the words he lived by. He observed every rite and ritual of his people. He fought his tribal enemies, sang his war songs and danced his war dances.

The year rolled by, weeks merged into months, winter into spring, until one glorious summer at daybreak, he wakened to the voice of his little wife calling him. 'It will be today,' she said proudly, standing beside him.

He sprang from his couch of wolf skins and looked out upon the coming day: the promise of what it would bring him seemed to breathe through all his forest world. He took her very gently by the hand and led her through the tangle of wilderness down to the the water's edge where Stanley Park now bends about Prospect Point.

'I must swim,' he told her.

'I must swim too,' she smiled, with the perfect understanding of two people living in harmony together. For, to them, the old custom was law – the custom that the parents of a coming child must swim until their flesh is so clean that a wild animal cannot scent their closeness. If the wild creatures of the forest have no fear of them, then, and only then, are they fit to become parents, for to scent a human is in itself a fearsome thing to all wild creatures.

So the two of them plunged into the waters of the Narrows as the grey dawn slipped up the eastern skies and all the forest awoke to the life of a new day. Presently he led her ashore, and smilingly she crept away under the giant trees.

'I must be alone,' she said. 'But come to me at sunrise; you will not find me alone then.'

He smiled too, and plunged back into the sea. He had to swim through this hour when his fatherhood was coming upon him. It was the law that he had to be clean, spotlessly clean, so that when his child looked out upon the world it would have the chance to live its own life clean. If he did not swim hour upon hour, his child would come to an unclean father.

As he swam happily to and fro, a canoe bearing four men headed up the Narrows. These men were giants in size, and the stroke of their paddles made huge eddies that boiled like the seething tides.

'Out of our way!' they cried as his lithe, copper-coloured body rose and fell with each stroke. He laughed at them, giants though they were, and answered that he could not cease his swimming at their demand.

'But cease you shall!' they commanded. 'We are agents of Sagalie Tyee, and we command you to make way!'

He stopped swimming and, lifting his head, defied them.

'I shall not stop, nor yet go ashore,' he cried, striking out once more to the middle of the channel.

'Do you dare to disobey?' they cried. 'We are men of the Sagalie Tyee. We can turn you into a fish or a tree or a stone for disobeying the Great Tyee.'

'I dare anything for the purity of my child,' he replied. 'I dare even the Sagalie Tyee himself.'

The four men were astonished. They consulted together, lit their pipes and sat in council. Never had they, men of the Sagalie Tyee, been defied before. Now, for the sake of an unborn child, they were being disobeyed.

The lithe young body still swam in the cool waters. Superstition held that should their canoe, or even their paddle blades touch a human being, their magic power would be lost. The handsome young chief swam directly in their course. They dared not run him down; if they did, they would become as other men.

While they were wondering what to do, there floated from out of the forest a faint, strange, compelling sound. They listened, and the young chief ceased his stroke as he listened too. The faint sound drifted out across the waters once more. It was the cry of a little child. Then one of the four men, he that steered the canoe, the strongest and tallest of them all, stood erect, stretched out his arms towards the rising sun, and chanted, not a curse on the young chief's head, but a promise of everlasting days and freedom from death.

'Because you have defied us, we promise this,' he chanted. 'You have put your child's future above all things, and for that the Sagalie Tyee commands us to make you a model for your tribe. You shall never die, but you shall stand through all the years to come, where all eyes can see you. You shall be a monument to Pure Fatherhood.'

The four men lifted their paddles and the handsome young chief swam ashore; as his feet touched the line where sea and land meet he was turned to stone.

Then the four men said, 'His wife and child must always be near him. They shall not die, but live forever.'

And they, too, were turned to stone.

If you walk in the woods near Siwash Rock you will see a large rock and a smaller one beside it. They are the shy bride-wife from the north and her hour-old baby beside her. And below them, at the margin of the waters, is a tall, grey column of stone that stands as a monument to one man's love for his unborn child.

# NINETEEN

# THE THREE TESTS

*The lands of the Sioux are located in what are now the states
of Dakota and Minnesota. The Dakota people, who tell this story,
are natives of this region.*

◆ In the lands of the Sioux, upon the right bank of what is now the Mississippi River in Dakota, there was once a village of the Dakota people. And in that village lived a young woman of great grace and beauty. So lovely was she that suitors came from far and near to win her love. But, besides being very beautiful, she was also extremely difficult to please: she set such hard tests for would-be lovers that none could win her heart.

Not far off in what is now the Missouri Valley lived a young brave who came to hear of the maid's great charms; and he made up his mind to woo and win her. The difficulty of the task did not daunt him, and he set off upon his journey full of determination.

On his way he climbed a hill and saw in the distance a mighty mountain. Imagine his surprise when that mountain suddenly crumbled to dust and a level plain appeared in its place. As he came closer, he noticed a man with a long rake levelling the soil.

Realizing the man was so strong he could move mountains, the young brave immediately invited him to join his quest; perhaps the Strong One could help him in his mission. The man agreed and on they went together.

They had not gone far when the young brave saw in the distance a man with great rocks tied to his ankles.

'Why have you tied these great stones to your ankles?' he asked.

'Oh,' replied the man, 'every time I chase buffalo, I run so fast I overtake and lose them; so I tie stones to my ankles to slow me down.'

The young suitor at once invited the Swift One to join him on his mission, and the fellow readily agreed.

The three companions were walking along when they spied two great lakes beside which sat a man who kept bowing his head to drink the water. Surprised that he did not quench his thirst, the young brave asked, 'Why do you sit there drinking so much water?'

'Because,' said the man, 'I can never drink enough water; once I have finished this lake, I shall start on the other.'

Straightaway, the young suitor invited the Thirsty One to join them on their mission. So now there were four companions walking along. They had not gone far when they noticed a man with his eyes raised to the sky. Curious to know why he was looking up, the young brave approached and asked, 'Why do you walk with your eyes turned skywards?'

'I have shot an arrow into the sky and am waiting for it to fall,' the man said.

Such a Skilful Archer could well be useful in their mission; so he, too, was invited to join the group.

Not long after, the band of companions was making its way through a forest when it came upon a strange sight: there before it was a man lying on the ground with his ear pressed to the soil.

'Friend,' asked the young brave, 'what are you doing?'

'I am listening to the plants breathing,' replied the man.

'Who knows,' thought the suitor, 'perhaps Keen Ear will be of help to me in my mission?'

So he, too, was invited to join the band.

In the course of time the six companions arrived at their destination, and the young brave explained his mission. The villagers shook their heads: did he not know how impossible was his task?

When they realized he would not be dissuaded, they led him and his companions to a great boulder that overshadowed the village.

'If you wish to win the beautiful maiden,' they said, 'you must first remove this boulder; it keeps the sunlight from us.'

'But that is impossible,' muttered the young brave in despair.

'Not so,' said the Strong One. 'Nothing could be simpler.'

So saying, he put his shoulder to the boulder and, with a terrible crash, it crumbled into many pieces, strewing rocks and stones across the plain.

For the second test, the villagers brought great baskets of food and cauldrons of water.

'You must eat every crumb and drink every last drop of water,' they said.

Being hungry, the travellers managed to consume all the food. But the poor suitor gazed sadly at the great cauldrons of water.

'Alas,' he said, 'no one can drink all that.'

'Not so,' said the Thirsty One. And in the twinkling of an eye, he had drunk it all, every last drop.

The villagers were amazed.

'But the last test is the hardest,' they declared.

At that, the lovely maiden herself stepped forward.

'You must run a race with me,' she said to the young brave. 'But I warn you: no one has ever beaten me. Should you do so, you will have passed the three tests and I shall marry you.'

Naturally, the young brave chose the Swift One for this test. As the runners started, the onlookers watched them until they disappeared out of sight, surprised that there was nothing between them. Gradually, however, the maid began to tire. She had never been challenged by such a fast runner, and she turned to the Swift One, saying:

'Come, let us rest awhile before we complete the final leg.'

The man agreed, but no sooner had he sat down than he fell asleep. The young woman seized her opportunity: she raced off back to the village, as hard as she could go.

In the meantime, the five companions were anxiously awaiting the return of the two runners. Great was their disappointment when they saw the woman come into sight on her own.

Keen Ear at once pressed his ear to the ground, listening hard.

Looking up, he told his companions:

'He is fast asleep. I can hear him snoring.'

At that the Skilful Archer stepped forward and loosed an arrow from his bow. So accurate was his aim that it just nipped the sleeper's nose as it landed, rousing him from his slumbers. At once he jumped to his feet, looking round for the woman. Realizing he had been tricked, he raced

away to try to catch up with her.

Just as she was about to pass the winning post he surged past her and won the race.

So the young brave had passed all three tests and, to the great rejoicing from his companions, he and the lovely maid were married. And the two lived together in peace and happiness, producing many children to tell their story throughout the nations of the Sioux.

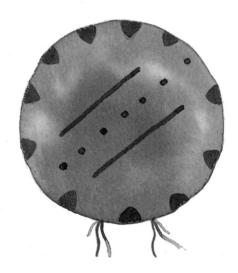

# TWENTY

# SEA SERPENT

*This is one of the legends collected from the Squamish people by Tekahionwake and included in her* Legends of Vancouver.

◆ We have lost many things. We have lost our lands, our forests, our fame, our fish. We have lost our ancient faith, our ancient dress; some of the younger people have even lost their language and the legends and traditions of their ancestors. We cannot call those old things back to us; they will never come again. We may travel many days up the mountain trails and look in the silent places for them. They are not there. We may paddle many moons upon the sea, but our canoes will never enter the channel that leads to the yesterdays of our people. These things are lost.

Yet there is one thing that we have never lost, for we have never had it. We were born without it. And among all the things we have learned from the white races this we have never acquired. It is greed.

We look upon the greed of gain and wealth accumulated above the head of poorer neighbours as one of the lowest sins to which a person may fall. It is thought disgraceful to have food if your neighbour has none. To be respected you must divide your possessions with your less fortunate fellows.

This is a legend about greed, here likened to a slimy sea serpent, the Salt-Chuck Oluk.

The story begins with the coming of the white gold hunters. They came with greedy, clutching fingers, greedy eyes, greedy hearts. The white men fought, murdered, starved, went mad with love of that gold far up the Fraser River. Tillicums were tillicums no more, brothers were foes, fathers and sons enemies. Their love of gold was a curse.

Many of our young men went as guides to the whites far up the Fraser. When they returned they brought back these tales of greed and murder, and our old people shook their heads and said evil would come of it. But all our young men, except one, returned as they went – kind to the poor, kind to those who were foodless, sharing whatever they had with their tillicums.

That one man was Shak-shak (the Hawk), who came back with hoards of gold nuggets, chickimin, everything. He was rich like the white men and, like them, he kept it all for himself. He would count his chickimin, count his nuggets, gloat over them, toss them from hand to hand. He rested his head on them when he slept, he carried them about with him throughout the day. He loved them better than food, better than his tillicums, better than life.

The whole tribe grew angry. They said Shak-shak had caught the disease of greed. To cure him of it he must give a great potlatch, share his riches with the poorer members of the tribe, divide them among the old, the sick, the foodless.

But he jeered and laughed and told them, 'No, no, no,' and went on loving and gloating over his gold.

It was then that the Sagalie Tyee spoke out of the sky:

'Shak-shak, you have made yourself a loathsome creature. You will not listen to the cry of the hungry, to the call of the old and sick, you will not share your possessions; you have made yourself an outcast from your tribe and you have disobeyed their ancient laws. Now I will make you a creature hated by all men, red and white. You will have two heads, for your greed has two mouths. One bites the poor, and one gnaws at your own evil heart. And the fangs in those mouths are poison – poison that kills the hungry and poison that kills your own manhood. Your evil heart will beat in the very centre of your foul body; and he that pierces it will kill the disease of greed for ever.'

When the sun rose above the North Arm next morning the people saw

a giant two-headed sea serpent stretched across the surface of the waters. They were horror-struck. They hated the creature, they feared and loathed it. Day after day it lay there, its monstrous heads lifted out of the waters, its mile-long body blocking the entrance to the Narrows and all outlets from the North Arm. The chiefs made council, the medicine men danced and chanted, but the Salt-Chuck Oluk never moved. It could not move, for it was the hated totem of what now ruled the white man's world – greed and love of chickimin. No one could ever move the love of chickimin from the white man's heart, no one could ever make him divide all he had with the poor.

But when the chiefs and medicine men had done all in their power, and still the Salt-Chuck Oluk lay across the waters, a handsome boy of some sixteen years approached them and reminded them of the words of the Sagalie Tyee:

'He who pierces the monster's heart will kill the disease of greed forever amongst his people.'

'Let me try to find this evil heart, O great men of my tribe,' he cried. 'Let me make war upon this creature. Let me rid my people of this pestilence.'

The boy was brave and handsome. His tribe called him the Tenas Tyee and they loved him. All his wealth of fish and furs, of game and hykwa he gave to the people who had none. He hunted for food for the old people. He tanned skins and furs for those whose feet were feeble, whose eyes were fading, whose blood ran thin with age.

'Let him go,' cried the people. 'This unclean monster can only be overcome by purity, this creature of greed can only be conquered by kindness. Let him go.'

The chiefs and medicine men listened, then consented.

'Go,' they commanded, 'and fight this thing with your strongest weapons – purity and kindness.'

Tenas Tyee turned to his mother.

'I shall be gone for several days,' he said. 'I shall be swimming all the time. While I am away put fresh furs on my bed each day, even if I am not here to lie upon them. If I know that my bed, my body and my heart are clean, I can overcome the serpent.'

'Your bed shall have fresh furs each morning,' promised his mother.

Tenas Tyee stripped off his clothes and, wearing only a buckskin belt into which he thrust his hunting knife, he flung himself into the water.

But at the end of several days he did not return. Now and then the people could see him swimming far out in mid-channel, trying to find the centre of the serpent where lay its evil, selfish heart. Finally, after many days, the people saw him rise out of the sea, climb to the summit of Brockton Point and greet the rising sun with outstretched arms.

Weeks went by. Months went by. And still Tenas Tyee swam each day searching for the heart of greed. And each morning the sunrise glinted on his slender copper-coloured body as he stood with outstretched arms at the summit of Brockton Point, greeting the coming day and then plunging from the peak into the sea.

At his home on the north shore his mother dressed his bed with fresh furs each morning. The seasons drifted by. Winter followed summer, summer followed winter. But it was four years before Tenas Tyee found the centre of the great Salt-Chuck Oluk and plunged his hunting knife into its heart. In its death agony it writhed through the Narrows, leaving a trail of blackness on the waters. Its huge body began to shrivel; it withered away

until nothing but the bones of its back remained; and they, sea-bleached and lifeless, soon sank to the ocean-bed miles away from the rim of land.

Yet as Tenas Tyee swam homeward and his clean young body crossed the black stain left by the serpent, the waters became clear and blue and sparkling. He had overcome even the black trail of the Salt-Chuck Oluk.

When at last he stood in the doorway of his home he spoke in clear, ringing tones:

'My mother, I could not have killed the monster of greed had you not helped me by keeping my bed fresh and clean, ready for my return.'

She looked at him as only mothers can.

'Each day, these four years past, I have laid fresh furs upon your bed. Sleep now and rest, my Tenas Tyee,' she said.

And that is the story of a white man's gift the red man never took.

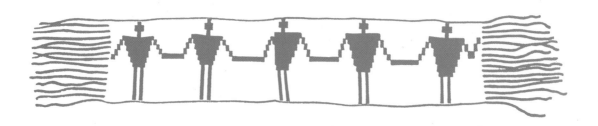

# GLOSSARY

chickimin (*Squamish*) – money

Great Tyee (*Slavey*) – head chief of the tribe

hogan (*Navajo*) – lodge, cabin, cave home

hykwa (*Squamish*) – large shells used as money

Kachinas (*Navajo*) – path of the spirits to heaven (the Milky Way); to the *Pueblo* peoples Kachinas are ancestral spirits, intermediaries between humans and gods

lodge – cabin usually made of pine logs with two smoke holes serving to admit air and expel smoke

Manitou (*Ojibway*) – spirit: either the supreme spirit, like the Gitche Manitou, or lesser spirits, like the Manitou of Bright Fire

orenda (*Mohawk*) – courage, spirit

poot-see (*Pahute*) – the stars

potlatch – celebration to give away possessions, to make gifts, so enhancing status

sachem (*Mohawk/Iroquois*) – tribal elder

Sagalie Tyee (*Coast Salish*) – the Great Spirit who instructs medicine men

shaman (*Pahute*) – the religious leader of a group

Skiikum Chuck (*Squamish*) – tumbling stream

Tenas Tyee (*Squamish/Salish*) – little or junior chief

tepee – conical tent made of skins, cloth or canvas on a frame of wooden poles

tillicum (*Squamish/Slavey/Salish*) – tribal brother or sister, close companion

Tirawa (*Pawnee*) – the Great Spirit (lit. 'Arch of Heaven')

wampum – beads made from shells and strung together for use as money or decoration, used to symbolize treaties and alliances

wigwam – hut or tent of skins, mats or bark on wooden poles

Yei (*Navajo*) – gods prominent in the world's creation and impersonated at certain ceremonies.

# SOURCES

I have not felt constrained by any written text, just as no storyteller keeps within the confines of a tale once told. Folk tales are spontaneous happenings that change with the season and passing fashion. Each telling is fresh and new. I have nonetheless tried to be faithful to the original storyline, the beliefs and locale.

What I have done is to consult as many collections as possible and to listen to live tellings and retellings. Out of the two, using a consistent style, comes the version in our book. The main sources consulted are as follows:

Emily Pauline Johnson, *Legends of Vancouver* (Macmillan Company of Canada, Toronto, 1961) for 'The Deep Waters', 'The Tulameen Trail', 'The Two Sisters', 'Sea Serpent', 'Siwash Rock' and 'Twins'. All these stories are from the tribes living in British Columbia, on the north-west coast of North America (the Squamish, Salish, Tsimsyan, Thompson, Slavey, etc.)

Ella Elizabeth Clark, *Indian Legends of Canada* (McClelland and Stewart, Toronto, 1960) for 'The Origin of Stories' (Seneca), 'The First White Water Lily' (Chippewa), 'Lone Bird' (Chippewa), and 'Great Snow in the Northlands' (Slavey, Dogrib).

Margaret Bemister, *Thirty Indian Legends of Canada* (J.J. Douglas, Vancouver, 1973) for 'Whispering Grass' (Ojibway), 'Spirits of the Evening Star' (Blackfoot) and 'Little Star' (Blackfoot).

William R. Palmer, *Why the North Star Stands Still and Other Indian Legends* (Zion Natural History Association, Springdale, 1973) for 'The Apache Cinderella' (Apache) and 'Why the North Star Stands Still' (Pahute).

Lewis Spence, *The Myths of the North American Indians* (George Harrap, London, 1914) for 'The Three Tests' (Sioux) and 'The Bear Man' (Pawnee).

C. Fayne Porter, *Our Indian Heritage* (The Chilton Book Company, Radnor, Pennsylvania) for 'Hiawatha' (Mohawk).

Cottie Burland, *North American Indian Mythology* (Harper and Row, New York, 1967) for 'Creation of the World' (Pueblo).

Dee Brown, *Bury My Heart at Wounded Knee* (Picador, London, 1979).